Scareware

Advanced Topics in Computer Security

Contents

Chapter 1

AV Security Suite

AV Security Suite is a piece of scareware and malware, or more specifically a piece of rogue security software, which poses as a pre-installed virus scanner on a victim's computer system. It is currently known to affect only Microsoft Windows systems, though may simply operate under a different name on other platforms to better fit in with their user-interfaces, as its disguise is a key component of its success. In the task manager it appears as a string a random characters that end with "tssd.exe" – an example is yvyvsggtssd.exe. It also can show a random string of characters that end with "shdw.exe".

1.1 Methods

After being installed on a target system, AV Security Suite sends out simulated virus alerts using pop-up windows that open from the rightmost section of the task bar. These notifications appear the same as those used by Windows itself, so can look genuine to a user not familiar with Windows' own style of reporting viruses (Windows Defender). AV Security Suite will show results of a fictitious virus scan,[1] this time using its own name, informing the user that their system is infected by viruses. Using a variety of different messages, some imitating Windows and some under the software's real name, it instructs the user to upgrade to the full version of AV Security Suite to remove the viruses. It then fakes the presence of unspecific viruses by performing actions such as preventing the opening of any programs (including Windows Task Manager)[2] and blocking internet connections. In essence, it renders a system almost useless. Since it is disguised as an anti-virus program, it is not considered to be a virus to any accessible anti-virus or anti-spyware programs.

1.2 Infection

AV Security Suite can infect computers using Adobe flash or other Adobe components found in regular websites, and so does not require voluntary download of software by the user. It has also been known to attack using Java software. There are currently no effective tools available to remove it, though some that claim to be able to do so are questionable in authenticity. Very few virus scanners are capable of detecting and removing the program. Norton and AVG Free Edition have been reported not to detect it. The paid edition of Malwarebytes' Anti-Malware has detected and removed it while the system is in safe mode, however a few months later the messages and program had come up again. While an operating system is infected, the malware will notify the user of infected system files and change the proxy server settings of the user's web browser so that the user will be under the false perception of no longer having Internet access. In addition, two websites that were not manufactured by the company will spontaneously pop up on the user's computer. One of these websites is for the erectile dysfunction drug Viagra, and the other is a pornographic website. Users are advised to dispose of the AV Security Suite virus immediately after their computer becomes infected, as the virus is possibly dangerous for younger users.

1.3   Removal

As the program will stop nearly all processes including shutting your computer down, the simplest removal method is to rebuild your computer from scratch using a previously made backup. The previously recommended method of restarting your computer in SAFE MODE rarely works with the more recent versions of this malware. Attempts to boot into SAFE MODE in newer versions usually result in a blue screen of death. If the user can get into SAFE MODE, they must search through the hidden system files (usually hidden to protect the user from accidentally deleting vital information from the system) and look for the malware manually. It will be disguised under an incoherent-looking string of letters and will not always include tssd.exe at the end.

Another alternative to these methods is to open the task manager immediately after booting the computer system and killing the process ending with "tssd.exe" or "shdw.exe" as soon as it appears under the list. After, one should restart their computer in safe mode and run a virus scanner, which will most likely detect the virus.

Alternatively, computers using multiple boots with a non-Windows operating system, such as most Linux distributions, can also access these files outside of Windows to delete them. Using a linux Live CD such as Ubuntu or Fedora is notably the most successful of these methods, as it can be booted from a CD drive instead of the hard drive.

As recently as October 2013, this virus could be successfully removed by taking a series of steps that while somewhat tedious to perform, did in fact work. The two primary keys to removal are 1) preventing the virus from communicating w/ the outside world by isolating its execution scope to only the infected PC and 2) preventing the virus from starting-up upon PC boot. A Windows 7 infected PC was completely freed/cleared of this virus by taking the following steps:

1. Force a hard shutdown of your infected PC by pressing on the power button for about 5 seconds or worst case, unplugging the power.

2. Prevent the PC from internet access by unplugging any internet cables and/or turning off wireless/WI-FI ability.

3. Start-up the PC - Windows 7 should recognize the previous hard shutdown and ask what you want to do. Select 'Start in Safe Mode with command prompt'. (Previous postings above indicate this "rarely works". That may be true in earlier Windows versions - in this case it worked).

4. At some point your PC should eventually display an old DOS-based Command Prompt window.

5. Type 'msconfig' on the line and hit 'Enter'. 'Normal Startup' will normally be selected. Change this to select 'Selective startup'.

6. Select the 'Startup' tab. You will see a list of programs that get started when your PC boots up. Somewhere in that list of checked items is the virus. In this case it was executing as 'avsecurity.exe' and had a Startup Item/Manufacturer named 'AVAST' or 'OVAST'. Please note that it may also be executing as 'avgsecurity.exe'.

7. Hover your mouse over the Location column. The hard drive location of the virus will appear on the screen. Make a note of its location (in this case it was under 'C:\ProgramData\avsecurity.exe').

8. Still on the 'Startup' tab, uncheck the checkbox under the Startup Item column and hit 'Apply', then 'OK' or 'Cancel'.

9. Now get rid of the virus executable. Type 'explorer' on the command line. This will start Windows File Explorer. Navigate to the hard drive location of the virus as noted in #7 above. Select the virus by clicking ONCE on the file (not TWICE! Double-clicking on the virus will start it up!). Right-click and select 'Delete' or hit your 'Delete' key on the keyboard and delete the virus program.

10. Now get rid of all the remnants of the virus from your registry (this step might actually be optional as the physical program virus has already been deleted from the system). Type 'regedit' on the command line. From the Registry Editor, select 'Edit' from the top menu and then select the 'Find' option. Type in 'InternetSecurity' as the search string. If/when found, some of the listed 'subkeys' should reference 'avsecurity'. The date/time stamp of the registry entry should also coincide with when your PC became infected. If/when found, right-click on the entry and select 'Delete'.

11. REMAIN DISCONNECTED FROM THE INTERNET and reboot your PC doing a "normal"/regular startup.

12. The virus should be gone and your PC should be functioning normally (unless the virus has resided so long on your PC and remained connected to the internet that the AVG Security virus has installed OTHER viruses on your PC).

13. If everything appears to be operating OK, start the Task Manager (right-click on the taskbar at the bottom of the

screen or type 'taskmgr' from a Run prompt).

14. Examine running Processes - avsecurity.exe as well as any 'tssd.exe' or 'shdw.exe' programs should not be seen.

15. Reconnect to the internet when ready.

Disclaimer: These steps may not work in all cases! The virus above was stopped (by a hard PC shutdown) and had its internet connection severed within 2 minutes of infection. It had very little time in which to do significant damage.
[3]

1.4 Developers

An analysis of the virus' graphical user interface, actions (dropping malware which attempts to send users to the same exact adult websites), and method of infection reveals it is likely that this piece of malware was developed, or at least inspired by, the same group which developed the fraudulent Antivirus System PRO, Antispyware Soft, Antivirus Center, and Antivirus Live, along with a number of other rogue antivirus applications. The claim on AV Security Suite's website, however, states that the developers of the program are based in London.

1.5 References

[1] BleepingComputer - AV Security Suite

[2] Virus Removal Guru - AV Security Suite

[3] Posted as expert in IBM mainframe and Windows PC software development and architecture and personal recent experience with this virus and its successful removal.

Chapter 2

Internet Security Essentials

Internet Security Essentials, also **InternetSecurityEssentials**, is a rogue security software pretending to protect the computer against malware and viruses. It is not to be confused with Webroot's "Webroot Internet Security Essentials" or "Microsoft Security Essentials".

2.1 Operation

As a fake antivirus program affecting Microsoft operating systems (Windows 9x, 2000, XP, Vista, Windows 7 and Windows 8) it installs itself through the use of a trojan horse from certain websites of the internet. Once downloaded and operating, it claims to find various viruses and malware on the computer that pose imminent danger scaring the user through pop-ups to buy its protection (scareware), while in reality the program itself is the malware. The virus was first encountered in February 2011. The program disrupts normal operations and should be removed immediately.

2.2 See also

- List of rogue security software

Chapter 3

List of rogue security software

The following is a partial list of rogue security software, most of which can be grouped into *families*. These are functionally identical versions of the same program repackaged as successive new products by the same vendor.[1][2]

3.1 References

[1] Stewart, Joe (2008-10-22), *Rogue Antivirus Dissected - Part 2*, SecureWorks

[2] Howes, Eric L (2008-11-21), *Spyware Warrior - Family Resemblances*, retrieved 2009-05-02

[3] Precise Security - Advanced Cleaner

[4] Kaspersky - AKM Antivirus 2010 Pro

[5] Spyware Warrior - AlfaCleaner

[6] Alpha AntiVirus - Spyware-Review

[7] BleepingComputer.com - ANG Antivirus

[8] Remove Antimalware Doctor - Spyware-Review

[9] 2 viruses - Remove Antimalware Pro

[10] Virus Removal Guru - AntiMalware GO

[11] Spyware-Fix - AntiMalware Go

[12] BleepingComputer - AntiSpyCheck 2.1

[13] BleepingComputer - AntispyStorm

[14] BleepingComputer - AntiSpyware 2008

[15] BleepingComputer - AntiSpyware Shield

[16] Virus Removal Guru - AntiSpyware Soft

[17] Precise Security - AntiSpywareSuite

[18] BleepingComputer - AntiVermins

[19] Virus Removal Guru - Antivir Solution Pro

[20] Spyware-Fix - Antivira AV

[21] BleepingComputer - Antivirii 2011

[22] Virus Removal Guru - Antivirus Action

[23] Virus Removal Guru - Antivirus Monitor

[24] BleepingComputer - Antivirus 7

[25] Remove Antivirus 8 - Spyware-Review

[26] Spyware-Fix - Antivirus 8

[27] BleepingComputer - Antivirus360

[28] BleepingComputer - Antivirus 2008

[29] Article noting that Antivirus 2010 and Anti-virus-1 are the same

[30] BleepingComputer - Antivirus 2010

[31] Symantec - AntiVirus Gold

[32] PCinDanger - Antivirus Live

[33] BleepingComputer - Antivirus Live

[34] BleepingComputer - Antivirus Master

[35] Spyware-Fix - Antivirus .NET

[36] BleepingComputer - AntivirusPro2009

[37] SpywareFixPro - Antivirus Pro 2010

[38] SpywareFixPro - Antivirus Pro 2010

[39] Remove-malware.net

[40] BleepingComputer - Antivirus Smart Protection

[41] BleepingComputer - Antivirus Soft

[42] Bleeping Computer - Antivirus Studio 2010

[43] BleepingComputer - Antivirus Suite

[44] remove-pcvirus.com - Antivirus Security Pro

[45] Faster, PC! Clean! Clean! - Antivirus System PRO

[46] Symantec - Antivirus XP

[47] MyAntispyware "How to remove Antivirus XP 2010"

[48] Spyware Fix - AV Antivirus Suite

[49] Spyware-Fix - AVG Antivirus 2011

[50] BleepingComputer - AV Security Essentials

[51] Virus Removal Guru - AV Security Suite

[52] SpywareRemove - Awola

[53] SpywareRemove - BestsellerAntivirus

[54] MyAntispyware "How to remove ByteDefender"

[55] Spyware-Fix - CleanThis

[56] BleepingComputer.com - Cloud Protection

[57] McAfee - ContraVirus

[58] Destroy Malware - Control Center

[59] SpywareFixPro - Cyber Security

[60] BleepingComputer - Data Protection

[61] Spyware-Fix - Defense Center

[62] Defru virus

[63] Sophos-Desktop Security 2010

[64] antivirus.about.com - "What is Disc Antivirsus Professional?"

[65] Spyware-Fix - Disk Doctor

[66] Spyware Fix Dr. Guard

[67] Symantec Symantec - DriveCleaner

[68] MalwareBytes - EasySpywareCleaner

[69] BleepingComputer - eco Antivirus

[70] Symantec - Errorsafe

[71] Destroy Malware - Essential Cleaner

[72] Markoff, John (May 30, 1989). "Virus Outbreaks Thwart Computer Experts". *The New York Times*. Retrieved April 3, 2010.

[73] Kabay, M. E. (August 17–23, 2005), "Some Notes on Malware", *Ubiquity* (New York: ACM) **6** (30), ISSN 1530-2180, OCLC 43723524, retrieved April 3, 2010

[74] Faster, PC! Clean! Clean! - GreenAV2009

[75] Spyware Fix - Hard Drive Diagnostic

[76] Spyware-Fix - HDD Fix

[77] Spyware-Fix - HDD Plus

[78] Virus Removal Guru - HDD Rescue

[79] Spyware Fix - HDD Rescue

[80] BleepingComputer - Home Security Solutions

[81] MalwareBytes - IEDefender

[82] SpywareRemove - InfeStop

[83] Symantec - Internet Antivirus

[84] Spyware Fix - Internet Antivirus 2011

[85] Spyware-Fix - Internet Defender 2011

[86] Precisesecurity.com

[87] PCindanger.com

[88] BleepingComputer - Internet Security 2011

[89] BleepingComputer - Internet Security 2012

[90] Virus Removal Guru - Internet Security Essentials

[91] BleepingComputer - Internet Security Guard

[92] BleepingComputer - Live PC Care

[93] MyAntispyware "How to remove Live Security Platinum"

[94] MyAntispyware "How to remove Live Security Suite"

[95] Bleeping Computer - Mac Defender

[96] Bleeping Computer - Mac Protector

[97] Symantec - MacSweeper

[98] MalwareBytes - Malware Alarm

[99] MalwareBytes - MalwareCore

[100] MalwareBytes - MalwareCrush

[101] BleepingComputer - Malware Defense

[102] Kaspersky - Malware Protection Center

[103] Spyware-Fix - Memory Fixer

[104] BleepingComputer MS Antispyware 2009

[105] BleepingComputer - MS Antivirus

[106] Spyware-Fix - MS Removal Tool

[107] Microsoft Windows Blog - Fake Microsoft Security Essentials

[108] Spyware Fix - My Security Engine

[109] Spyware Fix - My Security Shield

[110] BleepingComputer - My Security Wall

[111] Dunkelstern Software - Review

[112] Sunbelt Security - Netcom3 Cleaner

[113] BleepingComputer - Paladin Antivirus

[114] SpywareWarrior - PAL Spyware Remover

[115] BleepingComputer - PC Antispy

[116] MalwareBytes - PC Clean Pro

[117] SpywareRemove - PC Privacy Cleaner

[118] ComputerAssociates - PCPrivacy Tools

[119] Faster, PC! Clean! Clean! - PCSecureSystem

[120] MalwareBytes - PerfectCleaner

[121] BleepingComputer - Perfect Defender 2009

[122] BleepingComputer - PersonalAntiSpy Free

[123] BleepingComputer - Personal Antivirus

[124] Spyware-Fix - Personal Internet Security 2011

[125] Spyware Fix - Personal Security

[126] Malwarebytes - Personal Shield Pro

[127] SpywareRemove - PC Antispyware

[128] Spyware Fix - PC Defender Antivirus

[129] http://www.safebro.com/pckeeper-virus-remove

[130] BleepingComputer - Privacy Center

[131] BleepingComputer - Protection Center

[132] SpywareRemove - PSGuard

[133] Spyware-Fix - Quick Defragmenter

[134] BleepingComputer - Rapid AntiVirus

[135] BleepingComputer - Real Antivirus

[136] Precise Security - Registry Great

[137] Bleeping Computer - Safety Alerter 2006

[138] bleepingcomputer - remove-security-center

[139] SpywareFixPro - SafetyKeeper

[140] Emsi Soft - SaliarAR

[141] BleepingComputer - Secure Fighter

[142] SpywareRemove - SecurePCCleaner

[143] Bleeping Computer - SecureVeteran

[144] Spyware-Fix - Security Master AV

[145] BleepingComputer - Security Monitor 2012

[146] BleepingComputer - Security Protection

[147] Spywarevoid.com

[148] BleepingComputer - Security Scanner

[149] BleepingComputer - Security Shield

[150] BleepingComputer - Security Solution 2011

[151] Virus Removal Guru - Security Suite

[152] Spyware-Review Security Tool

[153] Spyware-Fix - Security Tool

[154] Precise Security - Security Toolbar 7.1

[155] PcinDanger - Security Essentials 2010

[156] http://botcrawl.com/slimcleaner-virus-removal/

[157] Remove the Smart Anti-Malware Protection Virus (Removal Guide) Bleeping Computer

[158] Virus Removal Guru - Smart Engine

[159] Virus Removal Guru - Smart HDD

[160] BleepingComputer - Smart Protection 2012

[161] http://malwaretips.com - ITExpert

[162] SpywareFixPro - Soft Soldier

[163] - Speedypc Pro

[164] Spyware Warrior - Spy Away

[165] Symantec

[166] BleepingComputer - SpyCrush

[167] Symantec - SpyDawn

[168] Youtube.com

[169] Precise Security - SpyGuarder

[170] BleepingComputer - SpyHeal

[171] Symantec - Spylocked

[172] Faster, PC! Clean! Clean! - SpyMarshal

[173] Symantec - SpyRid

[174] Symantec - SpySheriff

[175] Symantec - SpySpotter

[176] Should I Remove It - SpywareBot

[177] Spyware Warrior - Spyware Cleaner

[178] BleepingComputer - SpywareGuard 2008

[179] Javacool Blog - Fake "SpywareGuard2008? rogue – beware

[180] Faster, PC! Clean! Clean! - Spyware Protect 2009

[181] Symantec - Spyware Quake

[182] Spyware Warrior - Spyware Sheriff

[183] Sunbelt Security - Spyware Stormer

[184] Spyware Warrior - SpywareStrike

[185] MalwareBytes - Spyware Striker Pro

[186] McAfee - SpyWiper

[187] BleepingComputer - Super AV

[188] SysGuard

[189] Spyware Fix - Sysinternals Antivirus

[190] Faster, PC! Clean! Clean! - System Antivirus 2008

[191] MyAntispyware "How to remove SystemArmor"

[192] Remove System Check (Uninstall Guide)

[193] System Defender

[194] BleepingComputer - System Defragmenter

[195] Symantec - SystemDoctor

[196] BleepingComputer - System Live Protect

[197] - System Security

[198] System Tool Removal Guide

[199] Spyware-Fix - System Tool 2011

[200]

[201] Symantec - TheSpyBot

[202] Virus Removal Guru - ThinkPoint

[203] (aka total security) BleepingComputer - Total Secure 2009

[204] BleepingComputer - Total Win 7 Security

[205] BleepingComputer - Total Win Vista Security

[206] BleepingComputer - Total Win XP Security

[207] BleepingComputer - UltimateCleaner

[208] Spyware-Fix - Ultra Defragger

[209] Symantec - VirusHeat

[210] Symantec - VirusIsolator

[211] BleepingComputer - VirusLocker

[212] Symantec - VirusMelt

[213] Symantec - VirusProtectPro

[214] Sunbelt Security - Virus Ranger

[215] Symantec - VirusRemover2008

[216] ComputerAssociates - VirusRemover2009

[217] Virus Removal Guru - Virus Response Lab 2009

[218] BleepingComputer - VirusTrigger

[219] Spyware-Fix - Vista Antimalware 2011

[220] BleepingComputer Antivirus Vista 2010

[221] Virus Removal Guru - Vista Antispyware 2011

[222] Bleeping Computer Vista Antispyware 2012

[223] Precise Security - Vista Antivirus 2008

[224] Virus Removal Guru - Vista Home Security 2011

[225] BleepingComputer - Vista Internet Security 2012

[226] BleepingComputer - Vista Security 2011

[227] Destroy Malware - Vista Security 2012

[228] BleepingComputer - Vista Smart Security 2010

[229] BleepingComputer - Volcano Security Suite

[230] virus/remove-win7-antispyware-2011.html Spyware-Fix - Win7 Antispyware 2011

[231] MyAntispyware "How to remove Win Antispyware Center"

[232] Virus Removal Guru - Win 7 Home Security 2011

[233] Faster, PC! Clean! Clean! - WinAntiVirus Pro 2006

[234] Spyware-Fix - Win Defrag

[235] Virus Removal Guru - Windows 7 Recovery

[236] Precise Security - Windows Anticrashes Utility

[237] Bleeping Computer - Windows Antidanger Center

[238]

[239] Precise Security - Windows Attention Utility

[240] Precise Security - Windows Cleaning Tool

[241] Spyware-Fix - Windows Efficiency Magnifier

[242] Spyware-Fix - Windows Emergency System

[243] Windows Expert Console

[244] Spyware-Fix - Windows Passport Utility

[245] SpywareFixPro - Windows Police Pro

[246] Spyware-Fix - Windows Power Expansion

[247] Spyware-Fix - Windows Privacy Agent

[248] BleepingComputer - Windows Pro Rescuer

[249] Spyware-Fix - Windows Processes Organizer

[250] BleepingComputer - Windows Protection Suite

[251] BleepingComputer - Windows Protection Master

[252] Virus Removal Guru - Windows Recovery

[253] Spyware-Fix - Windows Remedy

[254] Spyware-Fix - Windows Repair

[255] Precise Security - Windows Restore

[256] BleepingComputer - Win 7 Security 2012

[257] Spyware-Fix - Windows Scan

[258] Kaspersky - Windows Shield Center

[259] Spyware-Fix - Windows Stability Center

[260] Bleeping Computer - Windows Steady Work

[261] Spyware-Fix - Windows Support System

[262] Bleeping Computer - Windows Tasks Optimizer

[263] Spyware-Fix - Windows Threats Removing

[264] Spyware-Fix - Windows Tool

[265] Bleeping Computer - Windows Tweaking Utility

[266] Spyware-Fix - Windows Utility Tool

[267] Virus Removal Guru - Windows Vista Recovery

[268] remove-pcvirus.com

[269] Bleepingcomputer.com

[270] Virus Removal Guru - Windows XP Recovery

[271] Symantec - WinFixer

[272] Spyware-Fix - Win HDD

[273] Symantec - WinHound

[274] Winpc Antivirus

[275] Winpc Defender

[276] Symantec - WinSpywareProtect

[277] BleepingComputer - WinWeb Security 2008

[278] Spyware Fix - Wireshark Antivirus

[279] Symantec - WorldAntiSpy

[280] Precise Security - XP Antimalware

[281] SpywareRemove - XP AntiSpyware 2009

[282] MyAntispyware - "How to remove XP AntiSpyware 2010"

[283] Bleeping Computer - XP Antispyware 2012

[284] BleepingComputer - XP Antivirus

[285] Destroy Malware - XP Antivirus 2012

[286] MyAntispyware "How to remove XP Antivirus Pro 2010"

[287] Bleeping Computer - XP Defender Pro

[288] Virus Removal Guru - XP Home Security 2011

[289] BleepingComputer - XP Internet Security 2010

[290] Destroy Malware - XP Security 2012

[291] MyAntspyware "How to remove XP Security Tool"

[292] Pandasecurity.com

[293] MyAntispyware "How to remove XJR Antivirus"

[294] BleepingComputer - Your Protection

[295] BleepingComputer - Your PC Protector

[296] Precise Security - Zinaps AntiSpyware 2008

[297] Security Shield Removal

Chapter 4

LizaMoon

LizaMoon is a piece of malware that infected thousands of websites beginning in September, 2010. It is an SQL injection attack that spreads scareware encouraging users to install needless and rogue "anti-virus software".[1] Although it does not use new infection techniques, it was initially thought to be notable based on the scale and speed at which it spread, and that it affected some of Apple's iTunes service. LizaMoon was initially reported to the general public by Websense Security Lab.[2]

4.1   Overview

Initial press statements reported the infection of hundreds of thousands or of millions of sites were infected. McAfee estimated approximately 1.5 million hosts affected between March and April 2011. However, subsequent research has shown a much lower infection rate. Although initial estimates for the infection based on Google search data were thought to show hundreds of thousands of infected sites, the true number appears to only be in the thousands: according to Niels Provos, a security researcher at Google, Google's safe browsing database indicates the LizaMoon attacks began around September 2010 and peaked in October 2010, with approximately 5600 infected sites.[3] Cisco researcher Mary Landesman has confirmed that the infection rate appears quite low.[4]

How the web sites spreading the infection were attacked remains a mystery. However, hackers may inject vulnerable and popular websites with malicious code in order to spread the infection once users visit these sites. Users should never permit installs of software of unknown provenance from the Internet under any circumstances – those that follow this policy cannot be infected by LizaMoon. These types of malware, known as rogue antivirus software, come under different names and logos such as "XP Security 2011", "Malware Scanner" or similar. After the initial installation, the software runs a fake scan showing non-existing malware on the system and in many cases requires the user to pay in order to remove the alleged malware.

4.2   Effects

As with all malware, LizaMoon is easier for a user to deal with by avoiding it rather than by attempting to repair the damage it causes after the fact. Fortunately, LizaMoon is easy for most users to avoid. The software requires the user to actively participate in downloading and installing itself. Indeed, to become infected, a user must give permission to the software four times. LizaMoon asks the user to install a piece of rogue antivirus software to remove various non-existent "viruses" from the PC. The rogue AV software that is installed is called Windows Stability Center. As of April 1, the file that is downloaded is currently detected by only 13 of 43 anti-virus engines according to VirusTotal.[5]

4.3 See also

4.4 References

[1] Stacy Cowley (2011-04-01). "LizaMoon attack infects millions of websites". *CNN Money*. Retrieved 2011-04-01.

[2] Reuters (2011-04-01). "Malicious Web attack hits a million site addresses". *Reuters*. Retrieved 2011-04-01.

[3] Provos, Niels. "Lizamoon SQL Injection Campaign Compared". Retrieved 7 April 2011.

[4] Landesman, Mary. "Lizamoon – Much Ado About Very Little". Retrieved 7 April 2011.

[5] Langa, Fred. "LizaMoon infection: a blow-by-blow account". Retrieved 7 April 2011.

4.4.1 Additional sources

- "LizaMoon breaking anti-virus barriers." CyberMedia India Online. Accessed October 2011.
- "Hackers infect websites to dupe Internet users." AFP. Accessed October 2011.

Chapter 5

Mac Shield

Mac Defender (also known as **Mac Protector**, **Mac Security**,[1]**Mac Guard**,[2] **Mac Shield**,[3] and **FakeMacDef**)[4] is an internet rogue security program that can be installed by unwitting users of computers running the Mac OS X operating system. The Mac security firm Intego discovered the fake antivirus software on 2 May 2011, with a patch not being provided by Apple until 31 May.[5] The software has been described as the first major malware threat to the Macintosh platform (although it does not attach to or damage any part of OS X).[6][7][8][9][10][11] However, it is not the first Mac-specific Trojan, and is not self-propagating.

5.1   Symptoms

Users typically encounter the program when opening an image found on a search engine. It appears as a pop-up indicating that viruses have been detected on the users' computer and suggests they download a program which, if installed, provides the users' personal information to unauthorized third parties.

The program appears in malicious links spread by search engine optimization poisoning on sites such as Google Image Search.[12] When a user accesses such a malicious link, a fake scanning window appears, originally in the style of a Windows XP application,[12] but later in the form of an "Apple-type interface".[13] The program falsely appears to scan the system's hard drive.[12] The user is then prompted to download a file that installs Mac Defender, and is then asked to pay US$59.95 to US$79.95 for a license for the software.[12][12] Rather than protect against viruses, Mac Defender hijacks the user's Internet browser to display sites related to pornography, and also exposes the user to identity theft (by passing on credit card information to the cracker).[12][14] A newer variant installs itself without needing the user to enter a password.[15] All variants require the user to actively click through an installer to complete installation even if a password is not required.[16]

5.2   Origin

The software has been traced through German websites, which have been closed down, to the Russian online payment ChronoPay. Mac Defender was traced to ChronoPay by the email address of ChronoPay financial controller Alexandra Volkova.[17] The email address appeared in domain registration for mac-defence.com and macbookprotection.com, two web sites Mac users are directed to in order to purchase the security software. ChronoPay is Russia's largest online payment processor. The web sites were hosted in Germany and were suspended by Czech registrar Webpoint.name. ChronoPay had earlier been linked to another scam in which users involved in file sharing were asked to pay a fine.[18][19]

5.3 Apple response

According to Sophos, by 24 May, 2011, there had been sixty thousand calls to AppleCare technical support about Mac Defender-related issues,[20] and Ed Bott of ZDNet reported that the number of calls to AppleCare increased in volume due to Mac Defender and that a majority of the calls at that time pertained to Mac Defender.[21] AppleCare employees were told not to assist callers in removing the software.[22] Specifically, support employees were told not to instruct callers on how to use Force Quit and Activity Monitor to stop Mac Defender, as well as not to direct callers to any discussions pertaining to the problems caused by Mac Defender.[20] An anonymous AppleCare support employee said that Apple instituted the policy in order to prevent users from relying on technical support instead of anti-virus programs.[22]

AppleCare employees were told not to assist callers in removing the software, but Apple later promised a software patch.[23] On 24 May 2011 Apple issued instructions on the prevention and removal of the malware.[24] The Mac OS X security update 2011-003 was released on 31 May 2011, and includes not only an automatic removal of the trojan, and other security updates, but a new feature that automatically updates malware definitions from Apple.[1]

On 31 May 2011 Apple released security update 2011-003, which addressed the threat and removed the trojan from any affected Mac computers, as well as adding a feature that automatically updated malware definitions from Apple.[1]

5.4 Mac Guard variant

A new variant of the program, Mac Guard, has been reported which does not require the user to enter a password to install the program,[25] although one still does have to run the installer.[26]

5.5 See also

- Leap (computer worm)
- Trojan BackDoor.Flashback
- Fakeflash

5.6 References

[1] "About Security Update 2011-003". 2011-05-31. Retrieved 31 May 2011.

[2] "Intego Mac Security Blog". 25 May 2001.

[3] "Mac malware morphs to 'MacShield'". *Technolog*. MSNBC. Retrieved 5 June 2011.

[4] "Threat Description: Rogue:OSX/FakeMacDef.A". F-Secure. Retrieved 11 February 2013.

[5] Hamburger, Ellis (2 May 2011). "WARNING: This Mac App Is Stealing Credit Card Numbers". Retrieved 7 December 2011.

[6] "Macs face first virus threat". techday.co.nz. 4 May 2011.

[7] "Say hello to MAC Defender, the first major widespread piece of Mac based malware". left-click.us.

[8] Dachis, Adam (25 May 2011). "How to Protect Your Computer from Mac Defender and Its Counterparts". *Mac Defender has been making a lot of noise as one of the first major Mac security threats.* lifehacker.com.

[9] Dan Moren (May 2, 2011). "New Mac Trojan horse masquerades as virus scanner". macworld.com.

[10] Trenholm, Rich (19 May 2011). "The old saw that Macs don't get viruses is under fire as a piece of malware called Mac Defender is rampaging across the Web". cnet.com.

[11] "Mac Defender fake antivirus software is first major attack on Apple computers". crave.cnet.co.uk.

[12] Wisniewski, Chester (2011-05-02). "Mac users hit with fake anti-virus when using Google image search". *Naked Security*. Sophos. Retrieved 24 May 2011.

[13] Mills, Elinor (2011-05-19). "How bad is the Mac malware scare? (FAQ)". *CNET*.

[14] Chen, Brian X. (2011-05-19). "New Mac Malware Fools Customers, But Threat Still Relatively Small". *Wired*. Condé Nast Digital. Retrieved 24 May 2011.

[15] "New Mac Defender Variant, MacGuard, Doesn't Require Password for Installation". The Mac Security Blog » INTEGO SECURITY MEMO.

[16] "New Mac Defender Variant, MacGuard, Doesn't Require Password for Installation". The Mac Security Blog » INTEGO SECURITY MEMO.

[17] "Apple takes on Mac Defender Scam". International Business Times. 29 May 2011.

[18] "MacDefender Scareware Linked to Russian Payment Site". *News & Opinion* (PCMag.com).

[19] "Russia's ChronoPay Executive Linked to Mac Defender Scam". *International Business Times*.

[20] Wisniewski, Chester (2011-05-24). "Apple support to infected Mac users: 'You cannot show the customer how to stop the process'". *Naked Security*. Sophos. Retrieved 24 May 2011.

[21] Bott, Ed (2011-05-18). "An AppleCare support rep talks: Mac malware is "getting worse"". *ZDNet*. Retrieved 24 May 2011.

[22] Cluley, Graham (2011-05-18). "Malware on your Mac? Don't expect AppleCare to help you remove it". *Naked Security*. Sophos. Retrieved 24 May 2011.

[23] "Mac malware authors release a new, more dangerous version". zdnet.com. 25 May 2011.

[24] "How to avoid or remove Mac Defender malware". 2011-05-24. Retrieved 1 June 2011.

[25] < "Mac Guard: Apple users hit by second Mac malware scam". *Christian Science Monitor Horizons blog*. 26 May 2001.

[26] "New Mac Defender Variant, MacGuard, Doesn't Require Password for Installation". Mac Security Blog from Intego. 25 May 2011.

Chapter 6

Mac Shield

Mac Defender (also known as **Mac Protector**, **Mac Security**,[1]**Mac Guard**,[2] **Mac Shield**,[3] and **FakeMacDef**)[4] is an internet rogue security program that can be installed by unwitting users of computers running the Mac OS X operating system. The Mac security firm Intego discovered the fake antivirus software on 2 May 2011, with a patch not being provided by Apple until 31 May.[5] The software has been described as the first major malware threat to the Macintosh platform (although it does not attach to or damage any part of OS X).[6][7][8][9][10][11] However, it is not the first Mac-specific Trojan, and is not self-propagating.

6.1 Symptoms

Users typically encounter the program when opening an image found on a search engine. It appears as a pop-up indicating that viruses have been detected on the users' computer and suggests they download a program which, if installed, provides the users' personal information to unauthorized third parties.

The program appears in malicious links spread by search engine optimization poisoning on sites such as Google Image Search.[12] When a user accesses such a malicious link, a fake scanning window appears, originally in the style of a Windows XP application,[12] but later in the form of an "Apple-type interface".[13] The program falsely appears to scan the system's hard drive.[12] The user is then prompted to download a file that installs Mac Defender, and is then asked to pay US$59.95 to US$79.95 for a license for the software.[12][12] Rather than protect against viruses, Mac Defender hijacks the user's Internet browser to display sites related to pornography, and also exposes the user to identity theft (by passing on credit card information to the cracker).[12][14] A newer variant installs itself without needing the user to enter a password.[15] All variants require the user to actively click through an installer to complete installation even if a password is not required.[16]

6.2 Origin

The software has been traced through German websites, which have been closed down, to the Russian online payment ChronoPay. Mac Defender was traced to ChronoPay by the email address of ChronoPay financial controller Alexandra Volkova.[17] The email address appeared in domain registration for mac-defence.com and macbookprotection.com, two web sites Mac users are directed to in order to purchase the security software. ChronoPay is Russia's largest online payment processor. The web sites were hosted in Germany and were suspended by Czech registrar Webpoint.name. ChronoPay had earlier been linked to another scam in which users involved in file sharing were asked to pay a fine.[18][19]

6.3 Apple response

According to Sophos, by 24 May, 2011, there had been sixty thousand calls to AppleCare technical support about Mac Defender-related issues,[20] and Ed Bott of ZDNet reported that the number of calls to AppleCare increased in volume due to Mac Defender and that a majority of the calls at that time pertained to Mac Defender.[21] AppleCare employees were told not to assist callers in removing the software.[22] Specifically, support employees were told not to instruct callers on how to use Force Quit and Activity Monitor to stop Mac Defender, as well as not to direct callers to any discussions pertaining to the problems caused by Mac Defender.[20] An anonymous AppleCare support employee said that Apple instituted the policy in order to prevent users from relying on technical support instead of anti-virus programs.[22]

AppleCare employees were told not to assist callers in removing the software, but Apple later promised a software patch.[23] On 24 May 2011 Apple issued instructions on the prevention and removal of the malware.[24] The Mac OS X security update 2011-003 was released on 31 May 2011, and includes not only an automatic removal of the trojan, and other security updates, but a new feature that automatically updates malware definitions from Apple.[1]

On 31 May 2011 Apple released security update 2011-003, which addressed the threat and removed the trojan from any affected Mac computers, as well as adding a feature that automatically updated malware definitions from Apple.[1]

6.4 Mac Guard variant

A new variant of the program, Mac Guard, has been reported which does not require the user to enter a password to install the program,[25] although one still does have to run the installer.[26]

6.5 See also

- Leap (computer worm)
- Trojan BackDoor.Flashback
- Fakeflash

6.6 References

[1] "About Security Update 2011-003". 2011-05-31. Retrieved 31 May 2011.

[2] "Intego Mac Security Blog". 25 May 2001.

[3] "Mac malware morphs to 'MacShield'". *Technolog*. MSNBC. Retrieved 5 June 2011.

[4] "Threat Description: Rogue:OSX/FakeMacDef.A". F-Secure. Retrieved 11 February 2013.

[5] Hamburger, Ellis (2 May 2011). "WARNING: This Mac App Is Stealing Credit Card Numbers". Retrieved 7 December 2011.

[6] "Macs face first virus threat". techday.co.nz. 4 May 2011.

[7] "Say hello to MAC Defender, the first major widespread piece of Mac based malware". left-click.us.

[8] Dachis, Adam (25 May 2011). "How to Protect Your Computer from Mac Defender and Its Counterparts". *Mac Defender has been making a lot of noise as one of the first major Mac security threats.* lifehacker.com.

[9] Dan Moren (May 2, 2011). "New Mac Trojan horse masquerades as virus scanner". macworld.com.

[10] Trenholm, Rich (19 May 2011). "The old saw that Macs don't get viruses is under fire as a piece of malware called Mac Defender is rampaging across the Web". cnet.com.

[11] "Mac Defender fake antivirus software is first major attack on Apple computers". crave.cnet.co.uk.

[12] Wisniewski, Chester (2011-05-02). "Mac users hit with fake anti-virus when using Google image search". *Naked Security*. Sophos. Retrieved 24 May 2011.

[13] Mills, Elinor (2011-05-19). "How bad is the Mac malware scare? (FAQ)". *CNET*.

[14] Chen, Brian X. (2011-05-19). "New Mac Malware Fools Customers, But Threat Still Relatively Small". *Wired*. Condé Nast Digital. Retrieved 24 May 2011.

[15] "New Mac Defender Variant, MacGuard, Doesn't Require Password for Installation". The Mac Security Blog » INTEGO SECURITY MEMO.

[16] "New Mac Defender Variant, MacGuard, Doesn't Require Password for Installation". The Mac Security Blog » INTEGO SECURITY MEMO.

[17] "Apple takes on Mac Defender Scam". International Business Times. 29 May 2011.

[18] "MacDefender Scareware Linked to Russian Payment Site". *News & Opinion* (PCMag.com).

[19] "Russia's ChronoPay Executive Linked to Mac Defender Scam". *International Business Times*.

[20] Wisniewski, Chester (2011-05-24). "Apple support to infected Mac users: 'You cannot show the customer how to stop the process'". *Naked Security*. Sophos. Retrieved 24 May 2011.

[21] Bott, Ed (2011-05-18). "An AppleCare support rep talks: Mac malware is "getting worse"". *ZDNet*. Retrieved 24 May 2011.

[22] Cluley, Graham (2011-05-18). "Malware on your Mac? Don't expect AppleCare to help you remove it". *Naked Security*. Sophos. Retrieved 24 May 2011.

[23] "Mac malware authors release a new, more dangerous version". zdnet.com. 25 May 2011.

[24] "How to avoid or remove Mac Defender malware". 2011-05-24. Retrieved 1 June 2011.

[25] < "Mac Guard: Apple users hit by second Mac malware scam". *Christian Science Monitor Horizons blog*. 26 May 2001.

[26] "New Mac Defender Variant, MacGuard, Doesn't Require Password for Installation". Mac Security Blog from Intego. 25 May 2011.

Chapter 7

Mac Shield

Mac Defender (also known as **Mac Protector**, **Mac Security**,[1]**Mac Guard**,[2] **Mac Shield**,[3] and **FakeMacDef**)[4] is an internet rogue security program that can be installed by unwitting users of computers running the Mac OS X operating system. The Mac security firm Intego discovered the fake antivirus software on 2 May 2011, with a patch not being provided by Apple until 31 May.[5] The software has been described as the first major malware threat to the Macintosh platform (although it does not attach to or damage any part of OS X).[6][7][8][9][10][11] However, it is not the first Mac-specific Trojan, and is not self-propagating.

7.1 Symptoms

Users typically encounter the program when opening an image found on a search engine. It appears as a pop-up indicating that viruses have been detected on the users' computer and suggests they download a program which, if installed, provides the users' personal information to unauthorized third parties.

The program appears in malicious links spread by search engine optimization poisoning on sites such as Google Image Search.[12] When a user accesses such a malicious link, a fake scanning window appears, originally in the style of a Windows XP application,[12] but later in the form of an "Apple-type interface".[13] The program falsely appears to scan the system's hard drive.[12] The user is then prompted to download a file that installs Mac Defender, and is then asked to pay US$59.95 to US$79.95 for a license for the software.[12][12] Rather than protect against viruses, Mac Defender hijacks the user's Internet browser to display sites related to pornography, and also exposes the user to identity theft (by passing on credit card information to the cracker).[12][14] A newer variant installs itself without needing the user to enter a password.[15] All variants require the user to actively click through an installer to complete installation even if a password is not required.[16]

7.2 Origin

The software has been traced through German websites, which have been closed down, to the Russian online payment ChronoPay. Mac Defender was traced to ChronoPay by the email address of ChronoPay financial controller Alexandra Volkova.[17] The email address appeared in domain registration for mac-defence.com and macbookprotection.com, two web sites Mac users are directed to in order to purchase the security software. ChronoPay is Russia's largest online payment processor. The web sites were hosted in Germany and were suspended by Czech registrar Webpoint.name. ChronoPay had earlier been linked to another scam in which users involved in file sharing were asked to pay a fine.[18][19]

7.3 Apple response

According to Sophos, by 24 May, 2011, there had been sixty thousand calls to AppleCare technical support about Mac Defender-related issues,[20] and Ed Bott of ZDNet reported that the number of calls to AppleCare increased in volume due to Mac Defender and that a majority of the calls at that time pertained to Mac Defender.[21] AppleCare employees were told not to assist callers in removing the software.[22] Specifically, support employees were told not to instruct callers on how to use Force Quit and Activity Monitor to stop Mac Defender, as well as not to direct callers to any discussions pertaining to the problems caused by Mac Defender.[20] An anonymous AppleCare support employee said that Apple instituted the policy in order to prevent users from relying on technical support instead of anti-virus programs.[22]

AppleCare employees were told not to assist callers in removing the software, but Apple later promised a software patch.[23] On 24 May 2011 Apple issued instructions on the prevention and removal of the malware.[24] The Mac OS X security update 2011-003 was released on 31 May 2011, and includes not only an automatic removal of the trojan, and other security updates, but a new feature that automatically updates malware definitions from Apple.[1]

On 31 May 2011 Apple released security update 2011-003, which addressed the threat and removed the trojan from any affected Mac computers, as well as adding a feature that automatically updated malware definitions from Apple.[1]

7.4 Mac Guard variant

A new variant of the program, Mac Guard, has been reported which does not require the user to enter a password to install the program,[25] although one still does have to run the installer.[26]

7.5 See also

- Leap (computer worm)
- Trojan BackDoor.Flashback
- Fakeflash

7.6 References

[1] "About Security Update 2011-003". 2011-05-31. Retrieved 31 May 2011.

[2] "Intego Mac Security Blog". 25 May 2001.

[3] "Mac malware morphs to 'MacShield'". *Technolog*. MSNBC. Retrieved 5 June 2011.

[4] "Threat Description: Rogue:OSX/FakeMacDef.A". F-Secure. Retrieved 11 February 2013.

[5] Hamburger, Ellis (2 May 2011). "WARNING: This Mac App Is Stealing Credit Card Numbers". Retrieved 7 December 2011.

[6] "Macs face first virus threat". techday.co.nz. 4 May 2011.

[7] "Say hello to MAC Defender, the first major widespread piece of Mac based malware". left-click.us.

[8] Dachis, Adam (25 May 2011). "How to Protect Your Computer from Mac Defender and Its Counterparts". *Mac Defender has been making a lot of noise as one of the first major Mac security threats*. lifehacker.com.

[9] Dan Moren (May 2, 2011). "New Mac Trojan horse masquerades as virus scanner". macworld.com.

[10] Trenholm, Rich (19 May 2011). "The old saw that Macs don't get viruses is under fire as a piece of malware called Mac Defender is rampaging across the Web". cnet.com.

[11] "Mac Defender fake antivirus software is first major attack on Apple computers". crave.cnet.co.uk.

[12] Wisniewski, Chester (2011-05-02). "Mac users hit with fake anti-virus when using Google image search". *Naked Security*. Sophos. Retrieved 24 May 2011.

[13] Mills, Elinor (2011-05-19). "How bad is the Mac malware scare? (FAQ)". *CNET*.

[14] Chen, Brian X. (2011-05-19). "New Mac Malware Fools Customers, But Threat Still Relatively Small". *Wired*. Condé Nast Digital. Retrieved 24 May 2011.

[15] "New Mac Defender Variant, MacGuard, Doesn't Require Password for Installation". The Mac Security Blog » INTEGO SECURITY MEMO.

[16] "New Mac Defender Variant, MacGuard, Doesn't Require Password for Installation". The Mac Security Blog » INTEGO SECURITY MEMO.

[17] "Apple takes on Mac Defender Scam". International Business Times. 29 May 2011.

[18] "MacDefender Scareware Linked to Russian Payment Site". *News & Opinion* (PCMag.com).

[19] "Russia's ChronoPay Executive Linked to Mac Defender Scam". *International Business Times*.

[20] Wisniewski, Chester (2011-05-24). "Apple support to infected Mac users: 'You cannot show the customer how to stop the process'". *Naked Security*. Sophos. Retrieved 24 May 2011.

[21] Bott, Ed (2011-05-18). "An AppleCare support rep talks: Mac malware is "getting worse"". *ZDNet*. Retrieved 24 May 2011.

[22] Cluley, Graham (2011-05-18). "Malware on your Mac? Don't expect AppleCare to help you remove it". *Naked Security*. Sophos. Retrieved 24 May 2011.

[23] "Mac malware authors release a new, more dangerous version". zdnet.com. 25 May 2011.

[24] "How to avoid or remove Mac Defender malware". 2011-05-24. Retrieved 1 June 2011.

[25] < "Mac Guard: Apple users hit by second Mac malware scam". *Christian Science Monitor Horizons blog*. 26 May 2001.

[26] "New Mac Defender Variant, MacGuard, Doesn't Require Password for Installation". Mac Security Blog from Intego. 25 May 2011.

Chapter 8

Mac Shield

Mac Defender (also known as **Mac Protector**, **Mac Security**,[1]**Mac Guard**,[2] **Mac Shield**,[3] and **FakeMacDef**)[4] is an internet rogue security program that can be installed by unwitting users of computers running the Mac OS X operating system. The Mac security firm Intego discovered the fake antivirus software on 2 May 2011, with a patch not being provided by Apple until 31 May.[5] The software has been described as the first major malware threat to the Macintosh platform (although it does not attach to or damage any part of OS X).[6][7][8][9][10][11] However, it is not the first Mac-specific Trojan, and is not self-propagating.

8.1   Symptoms

Users typically encounter the program when opening an image found on a search engine. It appears as a pop-up indicating that viruses have been detected on the users' computer and suggests they download a program which, if installed, provides the users' personal information to unauthorized third parties.

The program appears in malicious links spread by search engine optimization poisoning on sites such as Google Image Search.[12] When a user accesses such a malicious link, a fake scanning window appears, originally in the style of a Windows XP application,[12] but later in the form of an "Apple-type interface".[13] The program falsely appears to scan the system's hard drive.[12] The user is then prompted to download a file that installs Mac Defender, and is then asked to pay US$59.95 to US$79.95 for a license for the software.[12][12] Rather than protect against viruses, Mac Defender hijacks the user's Internet browser to display sites related to pornography, and also exposes the user to identity theft (by passing on credit card information to the cracker).[12][14] A newer variant installs itself without needing the user to enter a password.[15] All variants require the user to actively click through an installer to complete installation even if a password is not required.[16]

8.2   Origin

The software has been traced through German websites, which have been closed down, to the Russian online payment ChronoPay. Mac Defender was traced to ChronoPay by the email address of ChronoPay financial controller Alexandra Volkova.[17] The email address appeared in domain registration for mac-defence.com and macbookprotection.com, two web sites Mac users are directed to in order to purchase the security software. ChronoPay is Russia's largest online payment processor. The web sites were hosted in Germany and were suspended by Czech registrar Webpoint.name. ChronoPay had earlier been linked to another scam in which users involved in file sharing were asked to pay a fine.[18][19]

8.3   Apple response

According to Sophos, by 24 May, 2011, there had been sixty thousand calls to AppleCare technical support about Mac Defender-related issues,[20] and Ed Bott of ZDNet reported that the number of calls to AppleCare increased in volume due to Mac Defender and that a majority of the calls at that time pertained to Mac Defender.[21] AppleCare employees were told not to assist callers in removing the software.[22] Specifically, support employees were told not to instruct callers on how to use Force Quit and Activity Monitor to stop Mac Defender, as well as not to direct callers to any discussions pertaining to the problems caused by Mac Defender.[20] An anonymous AppleCare support employee said that Apple instituted the policy in order to prevent users from relying on technical support instead of anti-virus programs.[22]

AppleCare employees were told not to assist callers in removing the software, but Apple later promised a software patch.[23] On 24 May 2011 Apple issued instructions on the prevention and removal of the malware.[24] The Mac OS X security update 2011-003 was released on 31 May 2011, and includes not only an automatic removal of the trojan, and other security updates, but a new feature that automatically updates malware definitions from Apple.[1]

On 31 May 2011 Apple released security update 2011-003, which addressed the threat and removed the trojan from any affected Mac computers, as well as adding a feature that automatically updated malware definitions from Apple.[1]

8.4   Mac Guard variant

A new variant of the program, Mac Guard, has been reported which does not require the user to enter a password to install the program,[25] although one still does have to run the installer.[26]

8.5   See also

- Leap (computer worm)
- Trojan BackDoor.Flashback
- Fakeflash

8.6   References

[1] "About Security Update 2011-003". 2011-05-31. Retrieved 31 May 2011.

[2] "Intego Mac Security Blog". 25 May 2001.

[3] "Mac malware morphs to 'MacShield'". *Technolog*. MSNBC. Retrieved 5 June 2011.

[4] "Threat Description: Rogue:OSX/FakeMacDef.A". F-Secure. Retrieved 11 February 2013.

[5] Hamburger, Ellis (2 May 2011). "WARNING: This Mac App Is Stealing Credit Card Numbers". Retrieved 7 December 2011.

[6] "Macs face first virus threat". techday.co.nz. 4 May 2011.

[7] "Say hello to MAC Defender, the first major widespread piece of Mac based malware". left-click.us.

[8] Dachis, Adam (25 May 2011). "How to Protect Your Computer from Mac Defender and Its Counterparts". *Mac Defender has been making a lot of noise as one of the first major Mac security threats.* lifehacker.com.

[9] Dan Moren (May 2, 2011). "New Mac Trojan horse masquerades as virus scanner". macworld.com.

[10] Trenholm, Rich (19 May 2011). "The old saw that Macs don't get viruses is under fire as a piece of malware called Mac Defender is rampaging across the Web". cnet.com.

[11] "Mac Defender fake antivirus software is first major attack on Apple computers". crave.cnet.co.uk.

[12] Wisniewski, Chester (2011-05-02). "Mac users hit with fake anti-virus when using Google image search". *Naked Security*. Sophos. Retrieved 24 May 2011.

[13] Mills, Elinor (2011-05-19). "How bad is the Mac malware scare? (FAQ)". *CNET*.

[14] Chen, Brian X. (2011-05-19). "New Mac Malware Fools Customers, But Threat Still Relatively Small". *Wired*. Condé Nast Digital. Retrieved 24 May 2011.

[15] "New Mac Defender Variant, MacGuard, Doesn't Require Password for Installation". The Mac Security Blog » INTEGO SECURITY MEMO.

[16] "New Mac Defender Variant, MacGuard, Doesn't Require Password for Installation". The Mac Security Blog » INTEGO SECURITY MEMO.

[17] "Apple takes on Mac Defender Scam". International Business Times. 29 May 2011.

[18] "MacDefender Scareware Linked to Russian Payment Site". *News & Opinion* (PCMag.com).

[19] "Russia's ChronoPay Executive Linked to Mac Defender Scam". *International Business Times*.

[20] Wisniewski, Chester (2011-05-24). "Apple support to infected Mac users: 'You cannot show the customer how to stop the process'". *Naked Security*. Sophos. Retrieved 24 May 2011.

[21] Bott, Ed (2011-05-18). "An AppleCare support rep talks: Mac malware is "getting worse"". *ZDNet*. Retrieved 24 May 2011.

[22] Cluley, Graham (2011-05-18). "Malware on your Mac? Don't expect AppleCare to help you remove it". *Naked Security*. Sophos. Retrieved 24 May 2011.

[23] "Mac malware authors release a new, more dangerous version". zdnet.com. 25 May 2011.

[24] "How to avoid or remove Mac Defender malware". 2011-05-24. Retrieved 1 June 2011.

[25] < "Mac Guard: Apple users hit by second Mac malware scam". *Christian Science Monitor Horizons blog*. 26 May 2001.

[26] "New Mac Defender Variant, MacGuard, Doesn't Require Password for Installation". Mac Security Blog from Intego. 25 May 2011.

Chapter 9

Mac Shield

Mac Defender (also known as **Mac Protector**, **Mac Security**,[1]**Mac Guard**,[2] **Mac Shield**,[3] and **FakeMacDef**)[4] is an internet rogue security program that can be installed by unwitting users of computers running the Mac OS X operating system. The Mac security firm Intego discovered the fake antivirus software on 2 May 2011, with a patch not being provided by Apple until 31 May.[5] The software has been described as the first major malware threat to the Macintosh platform (although it does not attach to or damage any part of OS X).[6][7][8][9][10][11] However, it is not the first Mac-specific Trojan, and is not self-propagating.

9.1 Symptoms

Users typically encounter the program when opening an image found on a search engine. It appears as a pop-up indicating that viruses have been detected on the users' computer and suggests they download a program which, if installed, provides the users' personal information to unauthorized third parties.

The program appears in malicious links spread by search engine optimization poisoning on sites such as Google Image Search.[12] When a user accesses such a malicious link, a fake scanning window appears, originally in the style of a Windows XP application,[12] but later in the form of an "Apple-type interface".[13] The program falsely appears to scan the system's hard drive.[12] The user is then prompted to download a file that installs Mac Defender, and is then asked to pay US$59.95 to US$79.95 for a license for the software.[12][12] Rather than protect against viruses, Mac Defender hijacks the user's Internet browser to display sites related to pornography, and also exposes the user to identity theft (by passing on credit card information to the cracker).[12][14] A newer variant installs itself without needing the user to enter a password.[15] All variants require the user to actively click through an installer to complete installation even if a password is not required.[16]

9.2 Origin

The software has been traced through German websites, which have been closed down, to the Russian online payment ChronoPay. Mac Defender was traced to ChronoPay by the email address of ChronoPay financial controller Alexandra Volkova.[17] The email address appeared in domain registration for mac-defence.com and macbookprotection.com, two web sites Mac users are directed to in order to purchase the security software. ChronoPay is Russia's largest online payment processor. The web sites were hosted in Germany and were suspended by Czech registrar Webpoint.name. ChronoPay had earlier been linked to another scam in which users involved in file sharing were asked to pay a fine.[18][19]

9.3 Apple response

According to Sophos, by 24 May, 2011, there had been sixty thousand calls to AppleCare technical support about Mac Defender-related issues,[20] and Ed Bott of ZDNet reported that the number of calls to AppleCare increased in volume due to Mac Defender and that a majority of the calls at that time pertained to Mac Defender.[21] AppleCare employees were told not to assist callers in removing the software.[22] Specifically, support employees were told not to instruct callers on how to use Force Quit and Activity Monitor to stop Mac Defender, as well as not to direct callers to any discussions pertaining to the problems caused by Mac Defender.[20] An anonymous AppleCare support employee said that Apple instituted the policy in order to prevent users from relying on technical support instead of anti-virus programs.[22]

AppleCare employees were told not to assist callers in removing the software, but Apple later promised a software patch.[23] On 24 May 2011 Apple issued instructions on the prevention and removal of the malware.[24] The Mac OS X security update 2011-003 was released on 31 May 2011, and includes not only an automatic removal of the trojan, and other security updates, but a new feature that automatically updates malware definitions from Apple.[1]

On 31 May 2011 Apple released security update 2011-003, which addressed the threat and removed the trojan from any affected Mac computers, as well as adding a feature that automatically updated malware definitions from Apple.[1]

9.4 Mac Guard variant

A new variant of the program, Mac Guard, has been reported which does not require the user to enter a password to install the program,[25] although one still does have to run the installer.[26]

9.5 See also

- Leap (computer worm)
- Trojan BackDoor.Flashback
- Fakeflash

9.6 References

[1] "About Security Update 2011-003". 2011-05-31. Retrieved 31 May 2011.

[2] "Intego Mac Security Blog". 25 May 2001.

[3] "Mac malware morphs to 'MacShield'". *Technolog*. MSNBC. Retrieved 5 June 2011.

[4] "Threat Description: Rogue:OSX/FakeMacDef.A". F-Secure. Retrieved 11 February 2013.

[5] Hamburger, Ellis (2 May 2011). "WARNING: This Mac App Is Stealing Credit Card Numbers". Retrieved 7 December 2011.

[6] "Macs face first virus threat". techday.co.nz. 4 May 2011.

[7] "Say hello to MAC Defender, the first major widespread piece of Mac based malware". left-click.us.

[8] Dachis, Adam (25 May 2011). "How to Protect Your Computer from Mac Defender and Its Counterparts". *Mac Defender has been making a lot of noise as one of the first major Mac security threats.* lifehacker.com.

[9] Dan Moren (May 2, 2011). "New Mac Trojan horse masquerades as virus scanner". macworld.com.

[10] Trenholm, Rich (19 May 2011). "The old saw that Macs don't get viruses is under fire as a piece of malware called Mac Defender is rampaging across the Web". cnet.com.

[11] "Mac Defender fake antivirus software is first major attack on Apple computers". crave.cnet.co.uk.

[12] Wisniewski, Chester (2011-05-02). "Mac users hit with fake anti-virus when using Google image search". *Naked Security*. Sophos. Retrieved 24 May 2011.

[13] Mills, Elinor (2011-05-19). "How bad is the Mac malware scare? (FAQ)". *CNET*.

[14] Chen, Brian X. (2011-05-19). "New Mac Malware Fools Customers, But Threat Still Relatively Small". *Wired*. Condé Nast Digital. Retrieved 24 May 2011.

[15] "New Mac Defender Variant, MacGuard, Doesn't Require Password for Installation". The Mac Security Blog » INTEGO SECURITY MEMO.

[16] "New Mac Defender Variant, MacGuard, Doesn't Require Password for Installation". The Mac Security Blog » INTEGO SECURITY MEMO.

[17] "Apple takes on Mac Defender Scam". International Business Times. 29 May 2011.

[18] "MacDefender Scareware Linked to Russian Payment Site". *News & Opinion* (PCMag.com).

[19] "Russia's ChronoPay Executive Linked to Mac Defender Scam". *International Business Times*.

[20] Wisniewski, Chester (2011-05-24). "Apple support to infected Mac users: 'You cannot show the customer how to stop the process'". *Naked Security*. Sophos. Retrieved 24 May 2011.

[21] Bott, Ed (2011-05-18). "An AppleCare support rep talks: Mac malware is "getting worse"". *ZDNet*. Retrieved 24 May 2011.

[22] Cluley, Graham (2011-05-18). "Malware on your Mac? Don't expect AppleCare to help you remove it". *Naked Security*. Sophos. Retrieved 24 May 2011.

[23] "Mac malware authors release a new, more dangerous version". zdnet.com. 25 May 2011.

[24] "How to avoid or remove Mac Defender malware". 2011-05-24. Retrieved 1 June 2011.

[25] < "Mac Guard: Apple users hit by second Mac malware scam". *Christian Science Monitor Horizons blog*. 26 May 2001.

[26] "New Mac Defender Variant, MacGuard, Doesn't Require Password for Installation". Mac Security Blog from Intego. 25 May 2011.

Chapter 10

MS Antivirus (malware)

Not to be confused with Microsoft Anti-Virus or Microsoft Security Essentials.

MS Antivirus (also known as **Spyware Protect 2009**) is a scareware rogue anti-virus which claims to remove fake virus infections found on a computer running Microsoft Windows. It attempts to scam the user into purchasing a "full version" of the software.[1]

10.1 Names

Many clones of MS Antivirus that include slight variations have been distributed throughout the web. They are known as XP Antivirus,[2] Vitae Antivirus, Windows Antivirus, Win Antivirus, Antivirus Action, Antivirus Pro 2009, 2010,2017 or simply just Antivirus Pro, Antivirus 2007, 2008, 2009, 2010, 2011, and 360, AntiMalware GO, Internet Antivirus Plus, System Antivirus, Spyware Guard 2008 and 2009, Spyware Protect 2009, Winweb Security 2008, System Security, Malware Defender 2009, Ultimate Antivirus2008, Vista Antivirus, General Antivirus, AntiSpywareMaster, Antispyware 2008, XP AntiSpyware 2008, 2009 and 2010, Antivirus Vista 2010, Real Antivirus, WinPCDefender, Antivirus XP Pro, Anti-Virus-1, Antivirus Soft, Vista Antispyware 2012, Antispyware Soft, Antivirus System PRO, Antivirus Live, Vista Anti Malware 2010, Internet Security 2010, XP Antivirus Pro, Security Tool, VSCAN7, Total Security, PC Defender Plus, Disk Antivirus Professional, AVASoft Professional Antivirus, System Care Antivirus, and System Doctor 2014. Another MS Antivirus clone is named ANG Antivirus. This name is used to confuse the user of the software into thinking that it is the legitimate AVG Antivirus before downloading it.[3]

10.2 Symptoms of infection

Each variant has its own way of downloading and installing itself onto a computer. MS Antivirus is made to look functional to fool a computer user into thinking that it is a real anti-virus system in order to convince the user to "purchase" it. In a typical installation, MS Antivirus runs a scan on the computer and gives a false spyware report claiming that the computer is infected with spyware. Once the scan is completed, a warning message appears that lists the spyware 'found' and the user either has to click on a link or a button to remove it. Regardless of which button is clicked -- "Next" or "Cancel"—a download box will still pop up. This deceptive tactic is an attempt to scare the Internet user into clicking on the link or button to purchase MS Antivirus. If the user decides not to purchase the program, then they will constantly receive pop-ups stating that the program has found infections and that they should register it in order to fix them. This type of behavior can cause a computer to operate more slowly than normal.

MS Antivirus will also occasionally display fake pop-up alerts on an infected computer. These alerts pretend to be a detection of an attack on that computer and the alert prompts the user to activate, or purchase, the software in order to stop the attack. More seriously it can paste a fake picture of a Blue Screen of Death over the screen and then display a

**Internet Explorer Warning - visiting this web site may harm your computer!**

Most likely causes:

- The website contains exploits that can launch a malicious code on your computer
- Suspicious network activity detected
- There might be an active spyware running on your computer

What you can try:

- Purchase Spyware Protect 2009 for secure Internet surfing (Recommended).

- Check your computer for viruses and malware.

- More information

SWP '09 "protecting" the user from microsoft.com. Notice that the word type is different than what Internet Explorer usually uses.

fake startup image telling the user to buy the software. The malware may also block certain Windows programs that allow the user to modify or remove it. Programs such as Regedit can be blocked by this malware. The registry is also modified so the software runs at system startup. The following files may be downloaded to an infected computer:[4]

- MSASetup.exe

- MSA.exe

- MSA.cpl

- MSx.exe

Depending on the variant, the files have different names and therefore can appear or be labeled differently. For example, *Antivirus 2009* has the .exe file name a2009.exe.

In addition, in an attempt to make the software seem legitimate, MS Antivirus can give the computer symptoms of the "viruses" that it claims are on the computer.[5] For example, some shortcuts on the desktop may be changed to link to pornographic websites instead.

10.3 Malicious actions

Most variants of this malware will not be overtly harmful, as they usually will not steal a user's information (as spyware) nor critically harm a system. However, the software will act to inconvenience the user by frequently displaying popups that prompt the user to pay to register the software in order to remove non-existent viruses. Some variants are more harmful; they display popups whenever the user tries to start an application or even tries to navigate the hard drive, especially after the computer is restarted. It does this by modifying the Windows registry. This can clog the screen with repeated pop-ups, potentially making the computer virtually unusable. It can also disable real antivirus programs to protect itself from removal. Whichever variant infects a computer, MS Antivirus always uses system resources when running, potentially making an infected computer run more slowly than before.

The malware can also block access to known spyware removal sites and in some instances, searching for "antivirus 2009" (or similar search terms) on a search engine will result in a blank page or an error page. Some variants will also redirect the user from the actual Google search page to a false Google search page with a link to the virus' page that states that the user has a virus and should get Antivirus 2009. In some rare cases, with the newest version of the malware, it can prevent the user from performing a system restore.[6]

Antivirus 2009 can also disable legitimate anti-malware programs and prevent the user from opening or re-enabling them. Anti-malware applications disabled by Antivirus 2009 include McAfee, Spybot - Search & Destroy, AVG, Malwarebytes' Anti-Malware, and Superantispyware.

10.4 Earnings

In November 2008, it was reported that a hacker known as NeoN hacked the Bakasoftware's database, and posted the earnings of the company received from XP Antivirus. The data revealed the most successful affiliate earned USD$158,000 in a week.[7][8]

10.5 Court actions

On December 2, 2008 the U.S. District Court for the District of Maryland issued a temporary restraining order against Innovative Marketing, Inc. and ByteHosting Internet Services, LLC after receiving a request from the Federal Trade Commission (FTC). According to the FTC, the combined malware of WinFixer, WinAntivirus, DriveCleaner, ErrorSafe, and XP Antivirus has fooled over one million people into purchasing the software marketed as security products. The court also froze the assets of the companies in an effort to provide some monetary reimbursement to affected victims. The FTC claims the companies established an elaborate ruse that duped Internet advertising networks and popular Web sites into carrying their advertisements.

According to the FTC complaint, the companies charged in the case operated using a variety of aliases and maintained offices in the countries of Belize and Ukraine (Kiev). ByteHosting Internet Services is based in Cincinnati, Ohio. The complaint also names defendants Daniel Sundin, Sam Jain, Marc D'Souza, Kristy Ross, and James Reno in its filing, along with Maurice D'Souza, who is named relief defendant, for receiving proceeds from the scheme.[9]

10.6 See also

- Rogue software
- Adware
- Malware

10.7 References

[1] bleepingcomputer.com

[2] Seltzer, Larry. "MS Antivirus 2008 morphed from XP Antivirus 2008". *PC Magazine*.

[3] ANG AntiVirus 09 Remover at Spyware Removal Tools Accessed October 24, 2010

[4] http://www.ca.com/securityadvisor/pest/pest.aspx?id=453139480

[5] Vincentas (16 July 2013). "MS Antivirus in SpyWareLoop.com". Spyware Loop. Retrieved 28 July 2013.

[6] http://www.bleepingcomputer.com/malware-removal/remove-ms-antivirus

[7] Stewart, Joe (October 22, 2008). "Rogue Antivirus Dissected". SecureWorks, Inc. Archived from the original on 2010-03-09. Retrieved 8 March 2010.

[8] "Bakasoftware Russian Scareware Named and Shamed By Hacker". *IT Security NEWS*. SecPoint. 31 October 2008. Archived from the original on 2010-03-09. Retrieved 8 March 2010.

[9] "Court Halts Bogus Computer Scans". Federal Trade Commission. December 10, 2008. Retrieved 2009-01-19.

10.8   External links

- XP Antivirus 2009 Description and Removal instructions on About.com

Chapter 11

NightMare (scareware)

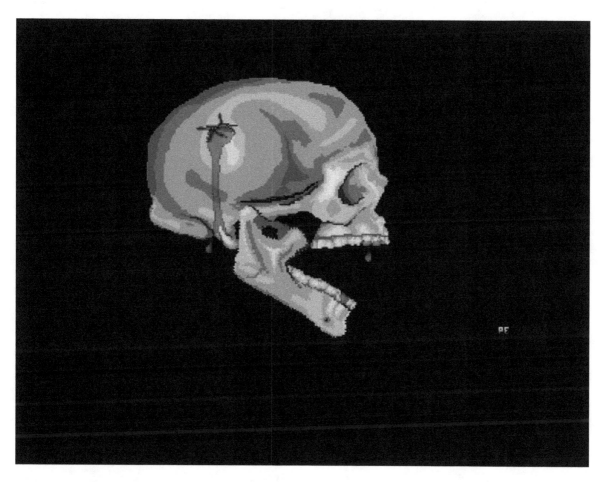

The image displayed every five minutes.

NightMare is a scareware program distributed on the Fish Disks for the Amiga computer (Fish #448). It is generally credited to be the first scareware program of its type.

The program was developed by Patrick Evans (Nobleton, Ontario, Canada) in 1990 and was free to redistribute, with source code available from the author.[1]

11.1 Effects

When NightMare executes, it runs in the background. Every five minutes, it changes the entire screen of the computer for four fifths of a second to an image of a skull with blood on its teeth and a bullet hole with blood leaking out of it, and plays a horrifying echoing shriek on the audio channels.[2]

11.2 References

[1] "Fish-disk 448 content: NightMare | Amiga Fish Disk database". Amiga-fish.erkan.se. 2013-09-30. Retrieved 2013-10-04.

[2] "Shields Up!: How to spot and avoid scareware". GadgeTell. Retrieved 2013-10-04.

Chapter 12

Registry cleaner

A **registry cleaner** is a class of third party software utility designed for the Microsoft Windows operating system, whose purpose is to remove redundant items from the Windows registry.

Registry cleaners are not supported by Microsoft, but vendors of registry cleaners claim that they are useful to repair inconsistencies arising from manual changes to applications, especially COM-based programs.

The effectiveness of registry cleaners is a controversial topic, with experts in disagreement over their benefits. The issue is further clouded by the fact that malware and scareware are often associated with utilities of this type.[1]

12.1 Advantages and disadvantages

Due to the sheer size and complexity of the registry database, manually cleaning up redundant and invalid entries may be impractical, so registry cleaners try to automate the process of looking for invalid entries, missing file references or broken links within the registry and resolving or removing them.[2]

The correction of an invalid registry key can provide some benefits; but the most voluminous will usually be quite harmless, obsolete records linked with COM-based applications whose associated files are no longer present.

12.1.1 Registry damage

Some registry cleaners make no distinction as to the severity of the errors, and many that do may erroneously categorize errors as "critical" with little basis to support it.[1] Removing or changing certain registry data can prevent the system from starting, or cause application errors and crashes.

It is not always possible for a third party program to know whether any particular key is invalid or redundant. A poorly designed registry cleaner may not be equipped to know for sure whether a key is still being used by Windows or what detrimental effects removing it may have. This may lead to loss of functionality and/or system instability,[3][4][5] as well as application compatibility updates from Microsoft to block problematic registry cleaners.[6] The Windows Installer CleanUp Utility was a Microsoft-supported utility for addressing Windows Installer related issues,[7][8]

12.1.2 Malware payloads

Registry cleaners have been used as a vehicle by a number of trojan applications to install malware, typically through social engineering attacks that use website popups or free downloads that falsely report problems that can be "rectified" by purchasing or downloading a registry cleaner.[9] The worst of the breed are products that advertise and encourage a "free" registry scan; however, the user typically finds the product has to be purchased for a substantial sum, before it will effect any of the anticipated "repairs". Rogue registry cleaners "WinFixer" have been ranked as one of the most prevalent pieces of malware currently in circulation.[10]

12.1.3   Scanners as scareware

Rogue registry cleaners are often marketed with alarmist advertisements that falsely claim to have pre-analyzed your PC, displaying bogus warnings to take "corrective" action; hence the descriptive label "scareware". In October 2008, Microsoft and the Washington attorney general filed a lawsuit against two Texas firms, Branch Software and Alpha Red, producers of the "Registry Cleaner XP" scareware.[11] The lawsuit alleges that the company sent incessant pop-ups resembling system warnings to consumers' personal computers stating "CRITICAL ERROR MESSAGE! - REGISTRY DAMAGED AND CORRUPTED", before instructing users to visit a web site to download Registry Cleaner XP at a cost of $39.95.

12.1.4   Metrics of performance benefit

On Windows 9x computers, it was possible that a very large registry could slow down the computer's start-up time. However this is less of an issue with NT-based operating systems (including Windows XP and Vista), due to a different on-disk structure of the registry, improved memory management and indexing.[12] Furthermore, versions of Windows prior to Server 2003 may fail to start up, if the registry and kernel files are unable to fit within the first 16M of memory.[13] Slowdown due to registry bloat is thus far less of an issue in modern versions of Windows.

Conversely, defragmenting the underlying registry files (e.g. using the free Microsoft-supported PageDefrag tool),[14] rather than attempting to clean the Registry's contents, has a measureable benefit and has therefore been recommended in the past by experts such as Mark Russinovich. (A form of defragmentation capability is built directly into Windows since Vista.)

The Windows Performance Toolkit is specifically designed to troubleshoot performance-related issues under Windows, and it does not include Registry cleaning as one of its optimizations.[15]

12.1.5   Undeletable registry keys

Most registry cleaners cannot repair scenarios such as undeletable registry keys caused by embedded null characters in their names; only specialized tools such as the RegDelNull utility (part of the free Sysinternals software) are able to do this.[16]

12.1.6   Recovery capability limitations

A registry cleaner cannot repair a registry hive that cannot be mounted by the system, making the repair via "slave mounting" of a system disk impossible.

A corrupt registry can be recovered in a number of ways that are supported by Microsoft (e.g. Automated System Recovery, from a "last known good" boot menu, by re-running setup or by using System Restore). "Last known good" restores the last system registry hive (containing driver and service configuration) that successfully booted the system.

12.1.7   Malware removal

These tools are also difficult to manage in a non-boot situation, or during an infestation, compared to a full system restore from a backup. In the age of rapidly evolving malware, even a full system restore may be unable to rid a hard drive of a bootkit.

Registry cleaners are likewise not designed for malware removal, although minor side-effects can be repaired, such as a turned-off System Restore. However, in complex scenarios where malware such as spyware, adware and viruses are involved, the removal of system-critical files may result.[17]

12.1.8 Application virtualization

A registry cleaner is of no use for cleaning registry entries associated with a virtualised application since all registry entries in this scenario are written to an application-specific virtual registry instead of the real one.[18] Complications of detailed interactions of real-mode with virtual also leaves the potential for incorrect removal of shortcuts and registry entries that point to "disappeared" files, and consequent confusion by the user of cleaner products. There is little competent information about this specific interaction, and no integration. In general, even if registry cleaners could be arguably considered safe in a normal end-user environment, they should be avoided in an application virtualization environment.

12.2 See also

- Utility software

12.3 References

[1] "Symantec Report on Rogue Security Software" (PDF). Symantec. 2009-10-28. Retrieved 2010-04-15.

[2] "What Is The Windows Registry And Why Should I Use A Registry Cleaner?". Solvusoft. Retrieved 15 December 2014.

[3] "Error: "Internet Explorer Script Error..." when scanning after running a registry cleanup utility". Symantec. October 2, 2002. Retrieved 2008-05-19.

[4] "The .NET Framework 2.0 SP1 installation fails on a computer that has the .NET Framework 2.0 installed and that is running Windows XP, Windows Server 2003, or Windows 2000". Microsoft. April 24, 2008. Retrieved 2008-05-19.

[5] "OL2000: Error Message: "Outlook Caused an Invalid Page Fault in Module Msvcrt.dll" When Creating an Appointment". Microsoft. November 5, 2003. Retrieved 2008-05-19.

[6] "August 2009 Windows Vista and Windows Server 2008 Application Compatibility Update". Microsoft. 2009-09-01. Retrieved 2009-09-25.

[7] "Free Utility: Windows Installer CleanUp Utility". Microsoft.

[8] "How do I uninstall Office 2003, Office 2007 or Office 2010 suites if I cannot uninstall it from Control Panel?". Microsoft. 2010-06-29. Retrieved 2010-09-23.

[9] "Fright Fight: Washington Attorney General leading battle against scareware with Microsoft" (Press release). Attorney General, Washington. 2008-09-29. Retrieved 2010-04-01.

[10] "WinFixer". StopBadware.Org. Retrieved 2008-06-21.

[11] Shiels, Maggie (2008-10-01). "Fighting the scourge of scareware". BBC News. Retrieved 2008-10-02.

[12] "Windows 2000 Registry: Latest Features and APIs Provide the Power to Customize and Extend Your Apps". Retrieved 2007-07-19.

[13] http://support.microsoft.com/kb/277222

[14] Lance Whitney (September 2007). "Utility Spotlight PageDefrag". Microsoft. Retrieved 2008-08-29.

[15] "Windows Performance Analysis Tools". Microsoft. Retrieved 2010-08-08.

[16] Mark Russinovich (2006-11-01). "RegDelNull v1.1". Retrieved 2008-12-08.

[17] Bryce Cogswell and Mark Russinovich (2006-11-01). "RootkitRevealer v1.71". Microsoft. Retrieved 2008-12-08.

[18] Anthony Kinney. "Getting Started with Microsoft Application Virtualization". Microsoft. Retrieved 2009-01-06.

Chapter 13

Rogue security software

Rogue security software is a form of malicious software and Internet fraud that misleads users into believing there is a virus on their computer, and manipulates them into paying money for a fake malware removal tool (that actually introduces malware to the computer). It is a form of scareware that manipulates users through fear, and a form of ransomware.[1] Rogue security software has become a growing and serious security threat in desktop computing in recent years (from 2008 on).[2]

13.1 Propagation

Rogue security software mainly relies on social engineering (fraud) to defeat the security built into modern operating system and browser software and install itself onto victims' computers.[2] A website may, for example, display a fictitious warning dialog stating that someone's machine is infected with a computer virus, and encourage them through manipulation to install or purchase scareware in the belief that they are purchasing genuine antivirus software.

Most have a Trojan horse component, which users are misled into installing. The Trojan may be disguised as:

- A browser plug-in or extension (typically toolbar)

- An image, screensaver or archive file attached to an e-mail message

- Multimedia codec required to play a certain video clip

- Software shared on peer-to-peer networks[3]

- A free online malware-scanning service[4]

Some rogue security software, however, propagate onto users' computers as drive-by downloads which exploit security vulnerabilities in web browsers, PDF viewers, or email clients to install themselves without any manual interaction.[3][5]

More recently, malware distributors have been utilizing SEO poisoning techniques by pushing infected URLs to the top of search engine results about recent news events.[6] People looking for articles on such events on a search engine may encounter results that, upon being clicked, are instead redirected through a series of sites[7] before arriving at a landing page that says that their machine is infected and pushes a download to a "trial" of the rogue program.[8][9] A 2010 study by Google found 11,000 domains hosting fake anti-virus software, accounting for 50% of all malware delivered via internet advertising.[10]

Cold-calling has also become a vector for distribution of this type of malware, with callers often claiming to be from "Microsoft Support" or another legitimate organization.[11]

40

13.2 Common Infection Vectors [12]

13.2.1 Black Hat SEO [13]

Black Hat search engine optimization (SEO) is a technique used to trick search engines into displaying malicious URLs in search results. The malicious webpages are filled with popular keywords in order to achieve a higher ranking in the search results. When the end user searches the web, one of these infected webpages is returned. Usually the most popular keywords from services such as Google Trends are used to generate webpages via PHP scripts placed on the compromised website. These PHP scripts will then monitor for search engine crawlers and feed them with especially crafted webpages that are then listed in the search results. Then, when the user searches for their keyword or images and clicks on the malicious link, they will be redirected to the Rogue security software payload.

13.2.2 Malvertising

Most websites usually employ third-party services for advertising on their webpages. If one of these advertising services is compromised,they may end up inadvertently infecting all of the websites using their service by showing advertising rogue security software.

13.2.3 Spam Campaigns

Spam messages that include malicious attachments, links to binaries and driveby download sites are another common mechanism for distributing Rogue security software. Spam emails are often sent with content associated with typical day-to-day activities such as parcel deliveries, or taxation documents, designed to entice users to click on links or run attachments. When users succumb to these kinds of social engineering tricks they are quickly infected either directly via the attachment, or indirectly via a malicious website. This is known as a driveby download. Usually in drive-by download attacks the malware is installed on the victim's machine without any interaction or awareness and occurs simply by visiting the website.

13.3 Operation

Once installed, the rogue security software may then attempt to entice the user into purchasing a service or additional software by:

- Alerting the user with the fake or simulated detection of malware or pornography.[14]

- Displaying an animation simulating a system crash and reboot.[2]

- Selectively disabling parts of the system to prevent the user from uninstalling the malware. Some may also prevent anti-malware programs from running, disable automatic system software updates and block access to websites of anti-malware vendors.[15]

- Installing actual malware onto the computer, then alerting the user after "detecting" them. This method is less common as the malware is likely to be detected by legitimate anti-malware programs.

- Altering system registries and security settings, then "alerting" the user.[16]

Developers of rogue security software may also entice people into purchasing their product by claiming to give a portion of their sales to a charitable cause. The rogue Green antivirus, for example, claims to donate $2 to an environmental care program for each sale made.[17]

Some rogue security software overlaps in function with scareware by also:

- Presenting offers to fix urgent performance problems or perform essential housekeeping on the computer.[14]

- Scaring the user by presenting authentic-looking pop-up warnings and security alerts, which may mimic actual system notices.[18] These are intended to use the trust that the user has in vendors of legitimate security software.[2]

Sanction by the FTC and the increasing effectiveness of anti-malware tools since 2006 have made it difficult for spyware and adware distribution networks—already complex to begin with[19]—to operate profitably.[20] Malware vendors have turned instead to the simpler, more profitable business model of rogue security software, which is targeted directly at users of desktop computers.[21]

Rogue security software is often distributed through highly lucrative affiliate networks, in which affiliates supplied with Trojan kits for the software are paid a fee for every successful installation, and a commission from any resulting purchases. The affiliates then become responsible for setting up infection vectors and distribution infrastructure for the software.[22] An investigation by security researchers into the Antivirus XP 2008 rogue security software found just such an affiliate network, in which members were grossing commissions upwards of $USD150,000 over 10 days, from tens of thousands of successful installations.[23]

13.4   Countermeasures

13.4.1   Private efforts

Law enforcement and legislation in all countries were very slow to react to the appearance of rogue security software even though it simply uses new technical means to carry out mainly old and well-established kinds of crimes. In contrast, several private initiatives providing discussion forums and lists of dangerous products were founded soon after the appearance of the first rogue security software. Some reputable vendors also began to provide lists of rogue security software, for example Kaspersky.[24] In 2005, the Anti-Spyware Coalition was founded, a coalition of anti-spyware software companies, academics, and consumer groups.

Many of the private initiatives were at first more or less informal discussions on general Internet forums, but some were started or even entirely carried out by individual people. The perhaps most famous and extensive one is the Spyware Warrior list of rogue/suspect antispyware products and websites by Eric Howes,[25] which has however not been updated since May 2007. The website recommends checking the following websites for new rogue anti-spyware programs, most of which are however not really new and are "simply re-branded clones and knockoffs of the same rogue applications that have been around for years"[26]

In December 2008, the US District Court for Maryland—at the request of the FTC—issued a restraining order against Innovative Marketing Inc, a Kiev-based firm producing and marketing the rogue security software products WinFixer, WinAntivirus, DriveCleaner, ErrorSafe, and XP Antivirus.[27] The company and its US-based web host, ByteHosting Internet Hosting Services LLC, had their assets frozen, were barred from using domain names associated with those products and any further advertisement or false representation.[28]

Law enforcement has also exerted pressure on banks to shut down merchant gateways involved in processing rogue security software purchases. In some cases, the high volume of credit card chargebacks generated by such purchases has also prompted processors to take action against rogue security software vendors.[29]

13.5   See also

- Anti-virus

- FraudTool

- List of rogue security software

- Scareware

- Technical support scam
- Winwebsec

13.6 References

[1] "Symantec Report on Rogue Security Software" (PDF). Symantec. 2009-10-28. Retrieved 2010-04-15.

[2] "Microsoft Security Intelligence Report volume 6 (July - December 2008)". Microsoft. 2009-04-08. p. 92. Retrieved 2009-05-02.

[3] Doshi, Nishant (2009-01-19), *Misleading Applications – Show Me The Money!*, Symantec, retrieved 2009-05-02

[4] Doshi, Nishant (2009-01-21), *Misleading Applications – Show Me The Money! (Part 2)*, Symantec, retrieved 2009-05-02

[5] "News Adobe Reader and Acrobat Vulnerability". blogs.adobe.com. Retrieved 25 November 2010.

[6] Vincentas (13 July 2013). "Rogue Security Software in SpyWareLoop.com". Spyware Loop. Retrieved 24 July 2013.

[7] Chu, Kian; Hong, Choon (2009-09-30), *Samoa Earthquake News Leads To Rogue AV*, F-Secure, retrieved 2010-01-16

[8] Hines, Matthew (2009-10-08), *Malware Distributors Mastering News SEO*, eWeek, retrieved 2010-01-16

[9] Raywood, Dan (2010-01-15), *Rogue anti-virus prevalent on links that relate to Haiti earthquake, as donors encouraged to look carefully for genuine sites*, SC Magazine, retrieved 2010-01-16

[10] Moheeb Abu Rajab and Luca Ballard (2010-04-13). "The Nocebo Effect on the Web: An Analysis of Fake Anti-Virus Distribution" (PDF). Google. Retrieved 2010-11-18.

[11] "Warning over anti-virus cold-calls to UK internet users". BBC News. Retrieved 7 March 2012.

[12] "Sophos Fake Antivirus Journey from Trojan tpna" (PDF)., ctbalarmsinbirmingham.co.uk

[13] "Sophos Technical Papers - Sophos SEO Insights". *sophos.com*.

[14] *"Free Security Scan" Could Cost Time and Money*, Federal Trade Commission, 2008-12-10, retrieved 2009-05-02

[15] Vincentas (11 July 2013). "Rogue Security Software in SpyWareLoop.com". Spyware Loop. Retrieved 28 July 2013.

[16] Vincentas (11 July 2013). "Rogue Anti-Spyware in SpyWareLoop.com". Spyware Loop. Retrieved 28 July 2013.

[17] "Cantalktech.com". *cantalktech.com*.

[18] "SAP at a crossroads after losing $1.3B verdict". Yahoo! News. 24 November 2010. Retrieved 25 November 2010.

[19] *Testimony of Ari Schwartz on "Spyware"* (PDF), Senate Committee on Commerce, Science, and Transportation, 2005-05-11

[20] Leyden, John (2009-04-11). "Zango goes titsup: End of desktop adware market". The Register. Retrieved 2009-05-05.

[21] Cole, Dave (2006-07-03), *Deceptonomics: A Glance at The Misleading Application Business Model*, Symantec, retrieved 2009-05-02

[22] Doshi, Nishant (2009-01-27), *Misleading Applications – Show Me The Money! (Part 3)*, Symantec, retrieved 2009-05-02

[23] Stewart, Joe (2008-10-22), *Rogue Antivirus Dissected - Part 2*, SecureWorks

[24] Rogue security software

[25] "Spyware Warrior: Rogue/Suspect Anti-Spyware Products & Web Sites". *spywarewarrior.com*.

[26] "Virus, Spyware, & Malware Removal Guides". *BleepingComputer*.

[27] *Ex Parte Temporary Restraining Order RDB08CV3233* (PDF), United States District Court for the District of Maryland, 2008-12-03, retrieved 2009-05-02

[28] Lordan, Betsy (2008-12-10), *Court Halts Bogus Computer Scans*, Federal Trade Commission, retrieved 2009-05-02

[29] Krebs, Brian (2009-03-20), "Rogue Antivirus Distribution Network Dismantled", *Washington Post*, retrieved 2009-05-02

13.7   External links

- Howes, Eric L (2007-05-04), *Spyware Warrior: Rogue/Suspect Anti-Spyware Products & Web Sites*, retrieved 2009-05-02

- Mariani, Brian L (2011-05-20), *Fake malware scanners:*, retrieved 2011-05-20

Chapter 14

Scareware

Not to be confused with careware or shareware.

Scareware is a form of malicious software that uses social engineering to cause shock, anxiety, or the perception of a threat in order to manipulate users into buying unwanted software. Scareware is part of a class of malicious software that includes rogue security software, ransomware and other scam software with malicious payloads, which have limited or no benefit to users, and are pushed by unethical marketing practices. Some forms of spyware and adware also use scareware tactics.

A tactic frequently used by criminals involves convincing users that a virus has infected their computer, then suggesting that they download (and pay for) fake antivirus software to remove it.[1] Usually the virus is entirely fictional and the software is non-functional or malware itself.[2] According to the Anti-Phishing Working Group, the number of scareware packages in circulation rose from 2,850 to 9,287 in the second half of 2008.[3] In the first half of 2009, the APWG identified a 585% increase in scareware programs.[4]

The "scareware" label can also apply to any application or virus (not necessarily sold as above) which pranks users with intent to cause anxiety or panic.

14.1 Scam scareware

Internet Security bloggers/writers use the term "scareware" to describe software products that produce frivolous and alarming warnings or threat notices, most typically for fictitious or useless commercial firewall and registry cleaner software. This class of program tries to increase its perceived value by bombarding the user with constant warning messages that do not increase its effectiveness in any way. Software is packaged with a look and feel that mimics legitimate security software in order to deceive consumers.[5]

Some websites display pop-up advertisement windows or banners with text such as: "Your computer may be infected with harmful spyware programs.[6] Immediate removal may be required. To scan, click 'Yes' below." These websites can go as far as saying that a user's job, career, or marriage would be at risk.[7] Products using advertisements such as these are often considered scareware. Serious scareware applications qualify as rogue software.

In recent findings, some scareware is not affiliated with any other installed programs. A user can encounter a pop-up on a website indicating that their PC is infected.[8] In some scenarios, it is possible to become infected with scareware even if the user attempts to cancel the notification. These popups are especially designed to look like they come from the user's operating system when they are actually a webpage.

A 2010 study by Google found 11,000 domains hosting fake anti-virus software, accounting for 50% of all malware delivered via internet advertising.[9]

Starting on March 29, 2011, more than 1.5 million web sites around the world have been infected by the LizaMoon SQL injection attack spread by scareware.[10][11]

Research by Google discovered that scareware was using some of its servers to check for internet connectivity. The data suggested that up to a million machines were infected with scareware.[12] The company has placed a warning in the search results of users whose computers appear to be infected.

14.1.1 Spyware

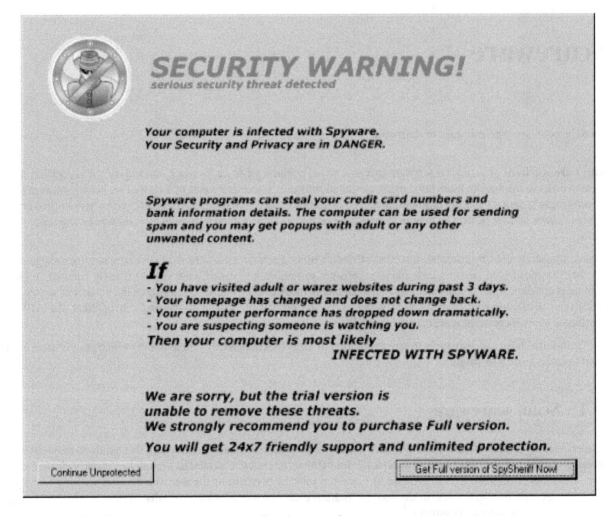

Dialog from SpySheriff, designed to scare users into installing the rogue software

Some forms of spyware also qualify as scareware because they change the user's desktop background, install icons in the computer's notification area (under Microsoft Windows), and generally make a nuisance of themselves, claiming that some kind of spyware has infected the user's computer and that the scareware application will help to remove the infection. In some cases, scareware trojans have replaced the desktop of the victim with large, yellow text reading "Warning! You have spyware!" or a box containing similar text, and have even forced the screensaver to change to "bugs" crawling across the screen. Winwebsec is the term usually used to address the malware that attacks the users of Windows operating system and produces fake claims similar to that of genuine anti-malware software.[13]

SpySheriff[14] exemplifies spyware/scareware: it purports to remove spyware, but is actually a piece of spyware itself, often accompanying SmitFraud infections. Other antispyware scareware may be promoted using a phishing scam.

Another example of scareware is Smart Fortress. This site scares people into thinking they have lots of viruses on their computer and asks them to buy the professional service.[15]

14.2   Uninstallation of security software

Another approach is to trick users into uninstalling legitimate antivirus software, such as Microsoft Security Essentials, or disabling their firewall.[16]

14.3   Legal action

In 2005, Microsoft and Washington State successfully sued Secure Computer (makers of Spyware Cleaner) for $1 million over charges of using scareware pop-ups.[17] Washington's attorney general has also brought lawsuits against Securelink Networks, High Falls Media, and the makers of Quick Shield.[18]

In October 2008, Microsoft and the Washington attorney general filed a lawsuit against two Texas firms, Branch Software and Alpha Red, producers of the Registry Cleaner XP scareware.[19] The lawsuit alleges that the company sent incessant pop-ups resembling system warnings to consumers' personal computers stating "CRITICAL ERROR MESSAGE! - REGISTRY DAMAGED AND CORRUPTED", before instructing users to visit a web site to download Registry Cleaner XP at a cost of $39.95.

On December 2, 2008, the U.S. Federal Trade Commission ("FTC") filed a Complaint in federal court against Innovative Marketing, Inc., ByteHosting Internet Services, LLC, as well as individuals Sam Jain, Daniel Sundin, James Reno, Marc D'Souza, and Kristy Ross. The Complaint also listed Maurice D'Souza as a Relief Defendant, alleged that he held proceeds of wrongful conduct but not accusing him of violating any law. The FTC alleged that the other Defendants violated the FTC Act by deceptively marketing software, including WinFixer, WinAntivirus, DriveCleaner, ErrorSafe, and XP Antivirus. According to the complaint, the Defendants falsely represented that scans of a consumer's computer showed that it is had been compromised or infected and then offered to sell software to fix the alleged problems.[20][21][22]

14.4   Prank software

Another type of scareware involves software designed to literally scare the user through the use of unanticipated shocking images, sounds or video.

- An early program of this type is NightMare, a program distributed on the Fish Disks for the Amiga computer (Fish #448) in 1991. When NightMare executes, it lies dormant for an extended (and random) period of time, finally changing the entire screen of the computer to an image of a skull while playing a horrifying shriek on the audio channels.[23]

- Anxiety-based scareware puts users in situations where there are no positive outcomes. For example, a small program can present a dialog box saying "Erase everything on hard drive?" with two buttons, both labeled "OK". Regardless of which button is chosen, nothing is destroyed other than the user's composure.[24]

- This tactic was used in an advertisement campaign by Sir-Tech in 1997 to advertise *Virus: The Game*. When the file is run, a full screen representation of the desktop appears. The software then begins simulating deletion of the Windows folder. When this process is complete, a message is slowly typed on screen saying "Thank God this is only a game." A screen with the purchase information appears on screen and then returns to the desktop. No damage is done to the computer during the advertisement.

14.5   See also

- Ransomware

- Rogue security software

- Winwebsec

14.6 Notes

[1] "Millions tricked by 'scareware'". BBC News. 2009-10-19. Retrieved 2009-10-20.

[2] 'Scareware' scams trick searchers. BBC News (2009-03-23). Retrieved on 2009-03-23.

[3] "Scareware scammers adopt cold call tactics". The Register. 2009-04-10. Retrieved 2009-04-12.

[4] Phishing Activity Trends Report: 1st Half 2009

[5] John Leydon (2009-10-20). "Scareware Mr Bigs enjoy 'low risk' crime bonanza". The Register. Retrieved 2009-10-21.

[6] Carine Febre (2014-10-20). "Fake Warning Example". Carine Febre. Retrieved 2014-11-21.

[7] "Symantec Security Response: Misleading Applications". Symantec. 2007-08-31. Retrieved 2010-04-15.

[8] JM Hipolito (2009-06-04). "Air France Flight 447 Search Results Lead to Rogue Antivirus". Trend Micro. Retrieved 2009-06-06.

[9] Moheeb Abu Rajab and Luca Ballard (2010-04-13). "The Nocebo Effect on the Web: An Analysis of Fake Anti-Virus Distribution" (PDF). Google. Retrieved 2010-11-18.

[10] content.usatoday.com

[11] reuters.com

[12] "Google to Warn PC Virus Victims via Search Site". BBC News. 2011-07-21. Retrieved 2011-07-22.

[13] Vincentas (11 July 2013). "Scareware in SpyWareLoop.com". Spyware Loop. Retrieved 27 July 2013.

[14] spywarewarrior.com filed under "Brave Sentry."

[15] "Smart Fortress 2012"

[16] theregister.co.uk

[17] Etengoff, Aharon (2008-09-29). "Washington and Microsoft target spammers". The Inquirer. Retrieved 2008-10-04.

[18] Tarun (2008-09-29). "Microsoft to sue scareware security vendors". *Lunarsoft*. Retrieved 2009-09-24. [...] the Washington attorney general (AG) [...] has also brought lawsuits against companies such as Securelink Networks and High Falls Media, and the makers of a product called QuickShield, all of whom were accused of marketing their products using deceptive techniques such as fake alert messages.

[19] "Fighting the scourge of scareware". BBC News. 2008-10-01. Retrieved 2008-10-02.

[20] "Win software". Federal Trade Commission.

[21] "Wanted by the FBI - SHAILESHKUMAR P. JAIN". FBI.

[22] "D'Souza Final Order" (PDF). Federal Trade Commission.

[23] Contents of disk #448. Amiga-stuff.com - see DISK 448.

[24] Dark Drive Prank

14.7 Further reading

- O'Dea, Hamish (2009-10-16). "The Modern Rogue – Malware With a Face". Australia: Microsoft.

14.8 External links

- Demonstration of scareware on YouTube
- The Case of the Unusable System
- Yes, that PC cleanup app you saw on TV at 3 a.m. is a waste

Chapter 15

Spylocked

SpyLocked, also known as **SpywareLocked**, is rogue software that seeks to trick the user into purchasing its full rogue version. SpyLocked issues false security messages alleging that the user's computer is infected with malicious spyware. Once installed, SpyLocked may be very difficult to remove and may re-install itself after partial removal.

15.1 Information

SpyLocked is a rogue security program that provides limited protection against spyware. It alerts users of false positives during spyware scans, as to goad them into purchase of the upgrade. SpyLocked's scans have also been shown to have a low accuracy, and to exaggerate low level threats as critical threats. The trial version will not remove these threats, and in order to do so the full version must be purchased.

15.2 Infection

SpyLocked's method of infection is similar to the delivery methods of all other rogue anti-spyware programs. SpyLocked can infect a computer through web browser security holes, downloading and installing itself through Zlob Trojan horses Infection.

15.3 General malicious characteristics and behavior

Some problems encountered with SpyLocked are:

- Poor scan reporting.

- False detection and misleading results.

- Deceptive advertising within application

- Fake critical infection alerts

- Self-updating

15.4   Problems caused by SpyLocked

Once inside the computer, SpyLocked may cause a variety of problems to the owner of the computer. Symptoms are obvious: popups, false system alerts in the notification area, and a noticeably slower computer. What are less obvious are the activities the software executes within the system. These trojans can steal personal information. These type of trojan have been known to steal bank account numbers, credit card information, home addresses, dial 1-900 numbers on your money, and much more.

- SpyLocked may generate excessive advertisements and bombard the computer screen with unwanted pop-ups.
- The infected computer may show an icon on the notification area adjacent to the system clock. Clicking the icon will take the user to a rogue anti-spyware site. Even if the message is not clicked, it will intermittently show a message similar to:

"The system has detected a number of active spyware applications that may impact on the performance of your computer. Click the icon to get rid of unwanted spyware by downloading an up-to-date anti-spyware solution."

- SpyLocked may not allow the user to uninstall it by using Add/Remove function and may recreate itself every time the user tries to remove it manually. Additionally, trying to remove it manually may even lead to a system crash. SpyLocked will deliver fake security messages that user's computer is infected with spyware in order to promote its alleged rogue anti-spyware product.
- SpyLocked may run as a number of different processes including 'isamain.exe', ismain.exe' and 'isamntr.exe' These processes usually can not be terminated individually (however, they can be removed using the 'End Process Tree' option on the Windows Task Manager) as they often restart themselves.
- SpyLocked may block the access to some websites for its purpose to prevent the user from downloading legitimate anti-spyware programs.

15.5   Variants

SpyLocked is known to be associated with such rogue anti-spyware programs as Spydawn, SpySheriff, SpywareQuake, VirusBurst, and VirusLocker. These programs share similar interface with the mentioned anti-spyware applications and have the same deceptive intentions.

15.6   Notes and references

- "SpyLocked" by Sunbelt Software

Chapter 16

SpywareStrike

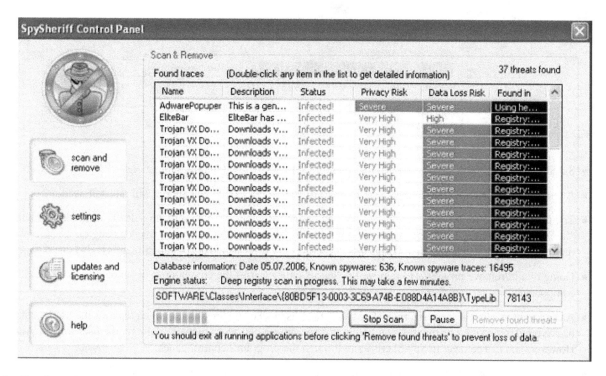

SpySheriff interface.

SpySheriff, also known as Brave Sentry, Pest Trap, SpyTrooper,[1] Spywareno, and MalwareAlarm,[2] is malware that disguises itself as an anti-spyware program. SpySheriff attempts to mislead a user into buying the program by repeatedly informing them of false threats to their system.[3] It is very difficult to remove SpySheriff from machines,[4] since it nests its components in System Restore folders, and also blocks some system management tools. Like all fake antiviruses, SpySheriff asks the user to register when they click <<Remove found threats>>. However, SpySheriff can be removed if the user has anti-malware tools on the machine, or owns a rescue disk.

16.1   Websites

SpySheriff used to be hosted at www.spy-sheriff.com[5] from 2005 to late 2008 and is now defunct. [6] Several typosquatted websites have also attempted to automatically install SpySheriff, including a fake version of Google.com (called Goggle.com). As of 2015, Goggle.com, which had changed ownership due to a lawsuit by Google, was a survey scam.

16.2   Problems caused by SpySheriff

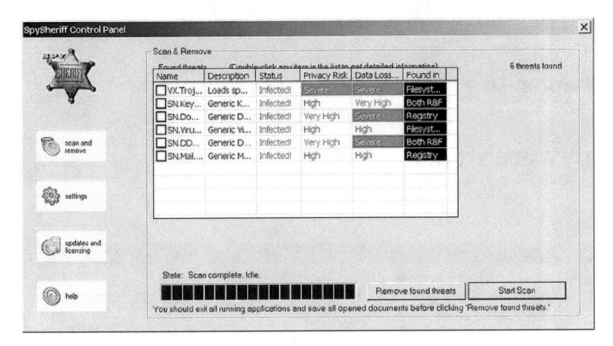

Another version of SpySheriff.

- SpySheriff reports false malware infections and pretends to detect real malware infections.[1][7]

- Attempts to remove SpySheriff have been reported to be unsuccessful as SpySheriff will reinstall itself.

- The desktop background may be replaced with an image resembling a blue screen of death, or a notice reading: "SPYWARE INFECTION! Your system is infected with spyware. Windows recommends that you use a spyware removal tool to prevent loss of data. Using this PC before having it cleaned of spyware threats is highly discouraged."

- Going to add/remove programs to remove SpySheriff either causes the computer to crash or does not remove all components.[8]

- Any attempt to connect to the Internet via a web browser is blocked by SpySheriff, which replaces the user's desktop background with a blue warning screen saying that the system has been stopped to protect the user from spyware. However, you can connect to Spy-Sheriff.com through the program's control panel.

- SpySheriff stops any attempt to do a system restore by causing the calendar and restore points to not load. This causes the user to be unable to revert their computer to an earlier state. A loop hole has been discovered, in that if the user undoes the last restore operation, the system will restore itself, allowing a chance to remove SpySheriff.[8]

- SpySheriff can detect certain running anti-spyware and anti-virus programs and disable them by ending their processes as soon as it detects them, preventing its detection and removal by these programs as long as it is active on the system.

- SpySheriff can disable the taskmgr or regedit tools that a user may attempt to bring up to end its active process or to remove its registry entries from Windows. Renaming the regedit and taskmgr executables will fool it, however.

16.3   See also

- Rogue security software
- Trojan horse (computing)

A fake infection warning pop-up.

16.4 References

[1] "SpySheriff Technical Details". Symantec. Retrieved 2009-11-01.

[2] "SpywareNo!". Retrieved 2009-11-11.

[3] "Spyware tunnels in on Winamp flaw". Joris Evers, CNET News.com, February 6, 2006. Retrieved 2009-11-01.

[4] "Top 10 rogue anti-spyware". Suze Turner, ZDNet, December 19, 2005. Retrieved 2009-11-01.

[5] "www.spysheriff.com". Internet Archive.

[6] "SunBelt Security Blog". Sunbelt Security. Retrieved 2009-11-01.

[7] Vincentas (18 October 2012). "spysheriff.exe in SpyWareLoop.com". Spyware Loop. Retrieved 27 July 2013.

[8] "SpySheriff - CA". CA. Archived from the original on April 5, 2007. Retrieved 2009-11-01.

16.5 External links

- Spy Sheriff Website at the Wayback Machine

- http://www.bleepingcomputer.com/forums/topic22402.html

- http://www.microsoft.com/security/portal/Threat/Encyclopedia/Entry.aspx?Name=Program%3aWin32%2fSpySheriff

Chapter 17

SpywareQuake

SpywareQuake is a fake anti-malware program for Microsoft Windows. It is commonly installed by Trojan Horse programs, but can be manually installed.

SpywareQuake's latest update was on February 13, 2007 at 11:49:07 AM. No later updates were ever recorded.[1]

17.1 References

[1] "SpywareQuake". Retrieved 2009-11-12.

Chapter 18

SpywareStrike

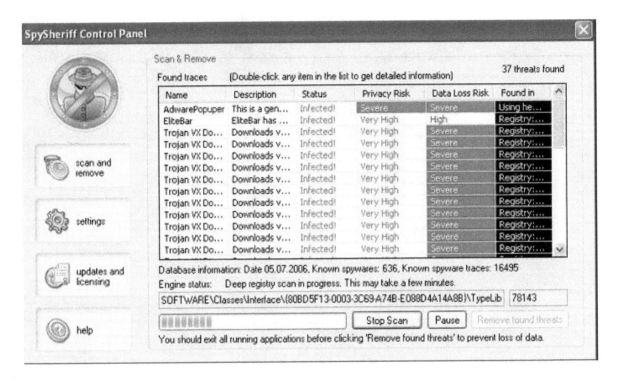

SpySheriff interface.

SpySheriff, also known as Brave Sentry, Pest Trap, SpyTrooper,[1] Spywareno, and MalwareAlarm,[2] is malware that disguises itself as an anti-spyware program. SpySheriff attempts to mislead a user into buying the program by repeatedly informing them of false threats to their system.[3] It is very difficult to remove SpySheriff from machines,[4] since it nests its components in System Restore folders, and also blocks some system management tools. Like all fake antiviruses, SpySheriff asks the user to register when they click <<Remove found threats>>. However, SpySheriff can be removed if the user has anti-malware tools on the machine, or owns a rescue disk.

18.1 Websites

SpySheriff used to be hosted at www.spy-sheriff.com[5] from 2005 to late 2008 and is now defunct. [6] Several typosquatted websites have also attempted to automatically install SpySheriff, including a fake version of Google.com (called Goggle.com). As of 2015, Goggle.com, which had changed ownership due to a lawsuit by Google, was a survey scam.

18.2   Problems caused by SpySheriff

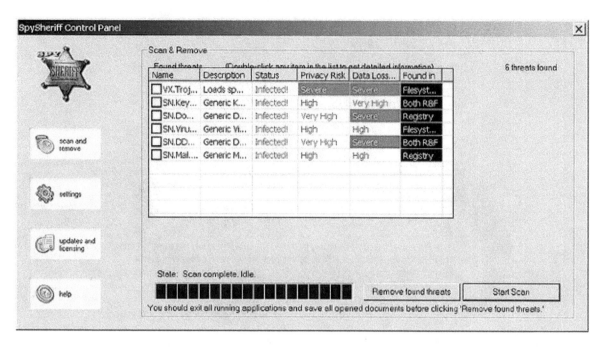

Another version of SpySheriff.

- SpySheriff reports false malware infections and pretends to detect real malware infections.[1][7]

- Attempts to remove SpySheriff have been reported to be unsuccessful as SpySheriff will reinstall itself.

- The desktop background may be replaced with an image resembling a blue screen of death, or a notice reading: "SPYWARE INFECTION! Your system is infected with spyware. Windows recommends that you use a spyware removal tool to prevent loss of data. Using this PC before having it cleaned of spyware threats is highly discouraged."

- Going to add/remove programs to remove SpySheriff either causes the computer to crash or does not remove all components.[8]

- Any attempt to connect to the Internet via a web browser is blocked by SpySheriff, which replaces the user's desktop background with a blue warning screen saying that the system has been stopped to protect the user from spyware. However, you can connect to Spy-Sheriff.com through the program's control panel.

- SpySheriff stops any attempt to do a system restore by causing the calendar and restore points to not load. This causes the user to be unable to revert their computer to an earlier state. A loop hole has been discovered, in that if the user undoes the last restore operation, the system will restore itself, allowing a chance to remove SpySheriff.[8]

- SpySheriff can detect certain running anti-spyware and anti-virus programs and disable them by ending their processes as soon as it detects them, preventing its detection and removal by these programs as long as it is active on the system.

- SpySheriff can disable the taskmgr or regedit tools that a user may attempt to bring up to end its active process or to remove its registry entries from Windows. Renaming the regedit and taskmgr executables will fool it, however.

18.3   See also

- Rogue security software

- Trojan horse (computing)

A fake infection warning pop-up.

18.4   References

[1] "SpySheriff Technical Details". Symantec. Retrieved 2009-11-01.

[2] "SpywareNo!". Retrieved 2009-11-11.

[3] "Spyware tunnels in on Winamp flaw". Joris Evers, CNET News.com, February 6, 2006. Retrieved 2009-11-01.

[4] "Top 10 rogue anti-spyware". Suze Turner, ZDNet, December 19, 2005. Retrieved 2009-11-01.

[5] "www.spysheriff.com". Internet Archive.

[6] "SunBelt Security Blog". Sunbelt Security. Retrieved 2009-11-01.

[7] Vincentas (18 October 2012). "spysheriff.exe in SpyWareLoop.com". Spyware Loop. Retrieved 27 July 2013.

[8] "SpySheriff - CA". CA. Archived from the original on April 5, 2007. Retrieved 2009-11-01.

18.5   External links

- Spy Sheriff Website at the Wayback Machine

- http://www.bleepingcomputer.com/forums/topic22402.html

- http://www.microsoft.com/security/portal/Threat/Encyclopedia/Entry.aspx?Name=Program%3aWin32%2fSpySheriff

Chapter 19

Tapsnake

Tapsnake is a scareware scam involving coercion to buy protection from a non-existent computer virus that has been distributed in various ways.[1]

It was offered as a game, malware/spyware included transmitting sundry information, particularly GPS location information to unauthorized third parties.

The name Tapsnake comes from the computer game Snaker, which has been revised such that the 'snake' responds to touchscreen taps by the user. The game is the front end of a trojan, spyware. An unsuspecting mobile device user is persuaded to load the "fun, free app," and then the person who wishes to monitor their movements must load a version which enables reception of location reports at 15-minute intervals.[2]

The most recent incarnation is enabled by activating a pop-up ad on an otherwise innocuous website. The user then receives dire warnings as to what the virus may do to them, is offered protection at a price via download (to a mobile device), and is promised increased speed and performance as an additional perk. Android seems to be the operating system most targeted, though iOS attacks are also threatened. The actual game and embedded spyware do not seem to be present at all in this scenario, except in the form of a threat. Blog-advisors seem to agree that the safest course of action is to simply close the advert, 'clicking' on as few things as possible. The intent is to coerce to defraud, in this instance, and not to monitor movement.

19.1   References

[1] Android Tapsnake Mobile Scareware: Ads Push Antivirus, by Satnam Narang, at Symantec; published December 20, 2013; retrieved April 6, 2015

[2] Tapsnake Infection: Not Very Likely, by David Harley, at Information Security Magazine; published January 29, 2015; retrieved April 6, 2015

Chapter 20

ThinkPoint

ThinkPoint (also known as Red Cross Antivirus, Peak Protection 2010, AntiSpy Safeguard, Major Defense Kit, Pest Detector, Privacy Guard 2010, and Palladium Pro) is a bogus virus/malware scanner, pretending to warn a user about threats and viruses "detected" by the scanner and is an impersonator of the real antivirus programs. It was created in August 2010.

The following message will be displayed if a user opens up a program scanned by the scanner:

> The application XXXXXXX.exe was launched successfully but it was forced to shut down due to security reasons.
> This happened because the application was infected by a malicious program which might pose a threat for the OS.
> It is highly recommended to install the necessary heuristic module and perform a full scan of your computer to exterminate malicious programs from it.

20.1   Payload

The payload starts when it deliberately closes the browser and appears as a fake Microsoft Security Essentials warning, asking the user to download an antivirus program and restart the computer to complete installation.

It will run automatically at system startup, running before Windows Explorer (thereby removing access to taskbar and icons until the program is closed). The ThinkPoint splash screen will appear, which has two buttons: "Normal Startup" (disabled) and "Safe Startup" (enabled) .

It has a Vista-like interface and uses the Windows logo. It will run a fake system scan and list a series of so-called "threats" detected after clicking on the "Safe Startup" button. It will then prompt the user to either buy a "heuristic program" or "continue unprotected." Usually, a user will choose "continue unprotected," but the same window will keep on appearing, leaving users no choice but to buy the program for USD $99.90. The program is known to block the Windows Task Manager, Windows Explorer, Google Chrome, and other programs that may terminate it. When a user presses the CTRL-ALT-DELETE or CTRL-SHIFT-ESC key combination, ThinkPoint will prevent it from starting and will display a window that reads: "The program taskmgr.exe is blocked due to safety issues which may pose a threat to the OS.

20.2   External links

- ThinkPoint Removal Instructions from BleepingComputer.com

- Microsoft Threat Encyclopedia

- The Win32 Fake PAV Virus and How it Works

- The Win32 Fake PAV Virus and How it Works

Chapter 21

Ultimate Defender

Ultimate Defender is a rogue antivirus program published by Nous-Tech Solutions Ltd. The program is considered malware due to its difficult uninstallation and deceptive operation.

21.1 Operation

The program may be obtained via free download. Once installed, it purports to search a user's computer for viruses and other spyware. During installation, however, other files are installed onto the computer. These files are then detected by the software and listed as critical threats requiring immediate removal. Users are prompted to upgrade to a full version of the software, which would be capable of removing the threat - despite the fact that the threat was installed with the software. [1]

In addition to its purported operation as an antivirus program, the software floods users with multiple false security warnings about threats to the security of files on the computer, overwhelming pop-up blockers such as Norton Antivirus. The software may also alter the operation of screen savers, desktop, and desktop icons, directing users to the software's homepage.

21.2 Removal

The software is related to Ultimate fixer and Ultimate Cleaner, in that the software is extremely difficult to remove once installed.[2] Companies such as Symantec provide detailed instructions for removal of the software, as some commercial anti-spyware programs may be unable to remove the software automatically. [3]

21.3 External links

- Video on YouTube

21.4 References

[1] Technical Data on Ultimate Defender software, accessed 12 September 2007

[2] Vincentas (9 July 2013). "Ultimate Defender in SpyWareLoop.com". Spyware Loop. Retrieved 28 July 2013.

[3] Removal Instructions for Ultimate Defender software, accessed 12 September 2007

Chapter 22

Ultimate Fixer

Ultimate Fixer was part of a spyware program that impersonated Windows Security Center.

Ultimate Fixer, along with Ultimate Cleaner and Ultimate Defender, were fake security programs for Windows.

Chapter 23

UltimateCleaner

UltimateCleaner 2007 was a rogue anti-spyware program that created fake Windows security messages and other security warnings in order to trick users into believing that computer was infected with spyware threats and that they needed to purchase the full version of UltimateCleaner 2007 to remove the threat.

23.1 See also

- Category:Spyware removal — programs which find and remove spyware
- Computer surveillance
- Adware
- Malware
- Trojan horse (computing)

23.2 Notes and references

- Information and Removal Instructions for UltimateCleaner
- Non-Techie Removal Guide for UltimateCleaner

Chapter 24

VirusProtectPro

VirusProtectPro is a rogue malware program that claims to be a commercial anti-spyware, when in fact it is, itself, adware-advertised. The software installs itself, without consent, on the user's computers and registry. It then sends messages such as "System Error, Buy this software to fix" or "Your System is infected with spyware, buy VirusProtectPro to clean it", redirecting the user to VirusProtectPro's homepage where he/she is prompted to buy the VirusProtectPro software.[1]

There are many variants of this rogue family including: AntiVirGear,[2] SpywareStrike, SpyFalcon, SpywareQuake, MalwareWipe, Spylocked, SpyDawn.

24.1 External links

- Free & Easy Removal Process
- Removal Instructions and Information
- More Removal Instructions
- Get Rid Of VirusProtectPro. Removal Method
- Video on YouTube

24.2 References

[1] Vincentas (25 October 2012). "VirusProtect 3.8 Website.lnk in SpyWareLoop.com". Spyware Loop. Retrieved 28 July 2013.

[2] "AntiVirGear Technical Overview". Symantec.

Chapter 25

WinFixer

WinFixer[n 1] is a family of scareware rogue security programs developed by Winsoftware which claim to repair computer system problems on Microsoft Windows computers if a user purchases the full version of the software. The software is mainly installed without the user's consent.[1] McAfee claims that "the primary function of the free version appears to be to alarm the user into paying for registration, at least partially based on false or erroneous detections."[2] The program prompts the user to purchase a paid copy of the program.[3]

The WinFixer web page (see the image) says it "is a useful utility to scan and fix any system, registry and hard drive errors. It ensures system stability and performance, frees wasted hard-drive space and recovers damaged Word, Excel, music and video files". However, these claims were never verified by any reputable source. In fact, most sources consider this program to actually reduce system stability and performance. The sites went defunct in December 2008 after actions taken by the Federal Trade Commission.

25.1   Installation methods

The WinFixer application is known to infect users using the Microsoft Windows operating system, and is browser independent. One infection method involves the Emcodec.E trojan, a fake codec scam. Another involves the use of the Vundo family of trojans.[4]

25.1.1   Typical infection

The infection usually occurs during a visit to a distributing web site using a web browser. A message appears in a dialog box or popup asking the user if they want to install WinFixer, or claiming a user's machine is infected with malware, and requests the user to run a free scan. When the user chooses any of the options or tries to close this dialog (by clicking 'OK' or 'Cancel' or by clicking the corner 'X'), it will trigger a pop-up window and WinFixer will download and install itself, regardless of the user's wishes.

25.1.2   "Trial" offer

A free "trial" offer of this program is sometimes found in pop-ups. If the "trial" version is downloaded and installed, it will execute a "scan" of the local machine, and a couple of non existent Trojans and viruses will be located, but does nothing else. To obtain a quarantine or removal, WinFixer requires the purchase of the program.[5] However, the alleged unwanted bugs are bogus, only serving to persuade the owner to buy the program.

Screenshot of the WinFixer homepage

25.1.3   WinFixer application

Once installed, WinFixer frequently launches pop-ups and prompts the user to follow its directions. Because of the intricate way in which the program installs itself into the host computer (including making dozens of registry edits),

An example of a WinFixer pop-up dialog box within Opera. Even if the Cancel or Close buttons were clicked to dismiss the box, it would redirect to a WinAntiVirus page anyway, featuring a simulated system scan.

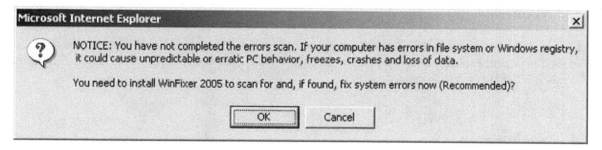

Initial message prior to infection - a user wishing to avoid infection might wish to disconnect from the Internet before closing the dialog box.

successful removal may take a fairly long time if done manually. When running, it can be found in the Task manager and stopped, but before long it will re-install and start up again.

WinFixer is also known to modify the Windows Registry, so that it launches automatically after reboot and scans the user's computer.[6]

25.1.4 Firefox popup

The Mozilla Firefox browser is vulnerable to initial infection by WinFixer. Once installed, WinFixer is known to exploit the SessionSaver extension for the Firefox browser. The program causes popups on every startup asking the user to download WinFixer, by adding lines containing the word 'WinFixer' to the prefs.js file.

25.1.5 Removal

The removal process of most rogue malware is often as simple as removing the directory it was originally installed into and then running basic cleanup software on the user's computer.

Unfortunately, simply deleting a directory won't remove WinFixer because it actively undoes whatever the user attempts. Frequently, the procedure that works on one system will not work on another because there are a large number of variants. Some sites provide manual techniques to remove infections that the automated tools can not remove.[7]

25.2   Domain ownership

The company that makes WinFixer, Winsoftware Ltd., claims to be based in Liverpool, England (Stanley Street, postcode: 13088.) However, this address has been proven false.[8]

The domain WINFIXER.COM on the whois database shows it is owned by a void company in Ukraine and another in Warsaw, Poland.[9] According to Alexa Internet, the domain is owned by Innovative Marketing, Inc., 1876 Hutson St, Honduras.

According to the public key certificate provided by GTE CyberTrust Solutions, Inc., the server *secure.errorsafe.com* is operated by ErrorSafe Inc. at 1878 Hutson Street, Belize City, BZ.

Running traceroute on Winfixer domains showed that most of the domains are hosted from servers at setupahost.net, which uses Shaw Business Solutions AKA Bigpipe as their backbone.

25.3   Technical information

25.3.1   Technical

WinFixer is closely related to Aurora Network's Nail.exe hijacker/spyware program. In worst-case scenarios, it may embed itself in Internet Explorer and become part of the program, thus being nearly impossible to remove. The program is also closely related to the Vundo trojan.[4][10]

25.4   Variants

25.4.1   Windows Police Pro

Windows Police Pro is a variant of WinFixer.[11] David Wood wrote in Microsoft TechNet that in March 2009, the Microsoft Malware Protection Center saw ASC Antivirus, the virus' first version. Microsoft did not detect any changes to the virus until the end of July that year when a second variant, Windows Antivirus Pro, appeared. Although multiple new virus versions have since appeared, the virus has been renamed only once, to Windows Police Pro. Microsoft added the virus to its Malicious Software Removal Tool in October 2009.[12]

The virus generates numerous persistent popups and messages displaying false scan reports intended to convince users that their computers are infected with various forms of malware that do not exist. When users attempt to close a popup message, they receive confirmation dialog boxes that switch the "Purchase full version" and "Continue evaluating" buttons.[12] Windows Police Pro generates a counterfeit Windows Security Center that warns users about the fake malware.[13]

Bleeping Computer and the syndicated "Propeller Heads" column recommended using Malwarebytes' Anti-Malware to remove Windows Police Pro permanently.[12][14] Microsoft TechNet and Softpedia recommended using Microsoft's Malicious Software Removal Tool to get rid of the malware.[12][15]

25.5   Effects on the public

25.5.1 Class action lawsuit

On September 29, 2006, a San Jose woman filed a lawsuit over WinFixer and related "fraudware" in Santa Clara County Superior Court, however, in 2007 the lawsuit was dropped. In the lawsuit, the plaintiffs charged that the WinFixer software "eventually rendered her computer's hard drive unusable. The program infecting her computer also ejected her CD-ROM drive and displayed Virus warnings." [16][17][18] KTVU (Channel 2 in Oakland, CA) carried a special report. [19]

25.5.2 Ads on Windows Live Messenger

On February 18, 2007, a blog called "Spyware Sucks" reported that the popular instant messaging application Windows Live Messenger had inadvertently promoted WinFixer by displaying a WinFixer advertisement from one of Messenger's ad hosts. [20] A similar occurrence also was reported on some MSN Groups pages. There were other reports before this one (one from Patchou, the creator of Messenger Plus!), and people had contacted Microsoft about the incidents. Whitney Burk from Microsoft issued this problem in his official statement:

25.5.3 Federal Trade Commission

On December 2, 2008, the Federal Trade Commission requested and received a temporary restraining order against Innovative Marketing, Inc., ByteHosting Internet Services, LLC, and individuals Daniel Sundin, Sam Jain, Marc D'Souza, Kristy Ross, and James Reno, the creators of WinFixer and its sister products. The complaint alleges that the products' advertising, as well as the products themselves, violate United States consumer protection laws. As of December 2008, this motion has attempted to halt the companies operations, and so halt the distribution of WinFixer and similar products offered by the same companies.[21] However, Innovative Marketing has flouted the court order and is currently being fined $8000 per day in civil contempt.[22]

On September 24, 2012, Kristy Ross was fined $163 million by the Federal Trade Commission for her part in this.[23][24] The article goes on to say that the WinFixer family of software was simply a con but does not acknowledge that it was in fact a program that made many computers unusable.

25.6 Notes

[1] Also known under various other names, including AVSystemCare, DriveCleaner, ECsecure, ErrorProtector, ErrorSafe, FreePC-Secure, Home Antivirus 20xx, PCTurboPro, Performance Optimizer, Personal Antivirus, PrivacyProtector, StorageProtector, SysProtect, SystemDoctor, VirusDoctor, WinAntiSpy, WinAntiSpyware, WinAntiVirusPro, Windows Police Pro, WinReanimator, WinSoftware, WinspywareProtect, XPAntivirus and Your PC Protector.

25.7 References

[1] "Winfixer". F-secure.com. Retrieved 2014-08-14.

[2] "Computer Virus Attacks, Information, News, Security, Detection and Removal | McAfee". Us.mcafee.com. Retrieved 2014-08-14.

[3] "WinFixer". Symantec. Retrieved 2014-08-14.

[4] "How to Remove WinFixer / Virtumonde / Msevents / Trojan.vundo". Bleepingcomputer.com. Retrieved 2014-08-14.

[5] Vincentas (July 6, 2013). "WinFixer in SpyWareLoop.com". Spyware Loop. Retrieved 2013-07-28.

[6] Archived November 18, 2007 at the Wayback Machine

[7] "WinFixer Virus Manual Removal - Vundo Variant". 2006.

[8] http://castlecops.com/t132998-quot_winfixer_quot_virus_quot_winsoftware_quot_crime_rin.html

[9] DNS Stuff: DNS tools, DNS hosting tests, WHOIS, traceroute, ping, and other network and domain name tools

[10]

[11] Long, Daniel (2009-10-02). "Fake Antivirus: 5 software titles you should definitely NOT install". *PC & Tech Authority* (nextmedia). Archived from the original on 2014-12-02. Retrieved 2014-12-02.

[12] Wood, David (2009-10-13). "Scanti-ly Clad - Another Rogue Stripped by MSRT". Microsoft TechNet. Archived from the original on 2014-11-13. Retrieved 2014-11-13.

[13] Abrams, Lawrence (2009-09-01). "Remove Windows Police Pro (Removal Guide)". Bleeping Computer. Archived from the original on 2014-11-15. Retrieved 2014-11-15.

[14] "Getting rid of malware". *Coeur d'Alene Press*. Propeller Heads. 2009-10-11. Archived from the original on 2014-11-11. Retrieved 2014-11-11.

[15] Oiaga, Marius (2009-10-15). "Windows Antivirus Pro Tackled by the Microsoft Malicious Software Removal Tool". Softpedia. Archived from the original on 2014-11-11. Retrieved 2014-11-11.

[16] Jeremy Kirk (March 8, 2007). "Lawyer sleuths out mystery around 'Winfixer'". Computerworld. Retrieved 2014-08-14.

[17] "Malware victim tries in vain to punish its source - San Jose Mercury News". Mercurynews.com. Retrieved 2014-08-14.

[18] "Lawsuit Filed Against Winfixer (a/k/a ErrorSafe, WinAntiSpyware, WinAntiVirus, SystemDoctor and DriveCleaner)". The Internet Patrol. Retrieved 2014-08-14.

[19] winfixerfixer. "Fraudware Special Report". YouTube. Retrieved 2014-08-14.

[20] Archived July 5, 2008 at the Wayback Machine

[21] "Court Halts Bogus Computer Scans". Federal Trade Commission (United States). December 10, 2008. Retrieved 2008-12-11.

[22] "Accused Scareware mongers held in contempt of court". The Register (United Kingdom). December 24, 2008. Retrieved 2008-12-24.

[23] Ionescu, Daniel (October 3, 2012). "Scareware con artist fined $163 million by FTC". techhive.com. Retrieved 2012-10-03.

[24] "Winfixer Opinion" (PDF). US Federal Trade Commission. September 24, 2012. Retrieved 2012-10-03.

25.8 External links

- McAfee's Entry on WinFixer

- Symantec's Entry on WinFixer and removal instructions

- Symantec's entry on ErrorSafe - a sister spyware application

- FTC complaint

25.9 Text and image sources, contributors, and licenses

25.9.1 Text

- **AV Security Suite** *Source:* https://en.wikipedia.org/wiki/AV_Security_Suite?oldid=641246124 *Contributors:* Red Jay, SmackBot, Lindenboy, Metallurgist, Stor~enwiki, Pbigio, Magioladitis, Sman789, Falcon8765, CowboySpartan, Acabashi, Leszek Jańczuk, Yobot, Bunnyhop11, DownAirStairsConditioner, Alzwded, Garverj, Mark Schierbecker, HamburgerRadio, Heymid, Noizekommando, ClueBot NG, King Of Aviators, WINAURW132, Excitium, Baska-cat, TriVista and Anonymous: 31

- **Internet Security Essentials** *Source:* https://en.wikipedia.org/wiki/Internet_Security_Essentials?oldid=532160517 *Contributors:* Ekem, SmackBot, Kinaro and Anonymous: 2

- **List of rogue security software** *Source:* https://en.wikipedia.org/wiki/List_of_rogue_security_software?oldid=700408902 *Contributors:* Discospinster, Smalljim, Lawrence King, Jobu, Chris the speller, Chris55, Fayenatic london, Geniac, Michael Goodyear, Kevinmon, Hbent, Drm310, Ignatzmice, Bonadea, Deor, Malcolmxl5, RJaguar3, France3470, Blanchardb, Socrates2008, Donsity, XLinkBot, NellieBly, Ben Ben, Lacrymocéphale, AnomieBOT, Addihockey10, James1011R, Stars1408, HamburgerRadio, Deadrat, Lotje, Punkofthedeath, John of Reading, TuneyLoon, Somebody500, Kunal0315, Rspence1234, WiiRocks566, Squady7, Roambassador, Zalchmen, ClueBot NG, Salmon92, Candlestick21, Guitarheroman202, Korrawit, Egg Centric, Asintro, Meltdown627, HappyLogolover2011, Fbacchin, Toxicgas1, Tonyjkent, Mark Arsten, Retireduser455656, Mikeshinobi1, BattyBot, Eduardofeld, Tangaling, Caaaake, EagerToddler39, Croberts pcd, Epicgenius, Froglich, Darth Occulus, Comp.arch, Vilmatech, OliviawithZiZi, Tonygoodmen, Bustedbrain16, Dsprc, Mamoth55, Heavy Punch, A8v, JackDaniels11, Zoethecomputergal, Rye Giggs, Jerodlycett, Acivon6791, PcSecAndy, Hfdhsdfhysfgadfgsadf, Dominic Hoe, Microsoftantivirus, EnigmaLord515 and Anonymous: 83

- **LizaMoon** *Source:* https://en.wikipedia.org/wiki/LizaMoon?oldid=633876190 *Contributors:* Discospinster, Pmetzger, Jjk, Ron Ritzman, Reisio, Sjö, Rjwilmsi, Brighterorange, Arthur Rubin, SmackBot, Magioladitis, Modal Jig, RJaguar3, Beeblebrox, AnomieBOT, Materialscientist, Jandalhandler, Torr3, Δ, Sexymax15, Northamerica1000, KScarfone, ChrisGualtieri and Anonymous: 9

- **Mac Defender** *Source:* https://en.wikipedia.org/wiki/Mac_Defender?oldid=697222709 *Contributors:* HangingCurve, StuartCheshire, RxS, Benlisquare, Bgwhite, RadioFan, Hydrargyrum, BorgQueen, SmackBot, Ph7five, Frap, Dl2000, Lenoxus, BeenAroundAWhile, CompRhetoric, Cydebot, Joe Schmedley, RJaguar3, Wikievil666, John Nevard, Eik Corell, Addbot, Fluffernutter, Freikorp, AnomieBOT, Xqbot, FrescoBot, Smile4ever, Eric 324, RedBot, Lotje, RjwilmsiBot, ZéroBot, Medeis, Wingman417, Champion, HandsomeFella, Kenny Strawn, ClueBot NG, Zashitnik, Island Monkey, JasonMashak, The Anonymouse, Zergeist and Anonymous: 19

- **Mac Guard** *Source:* https://en.wikipedia.org/wiki/Mac_Defender?oldid=697222709 *Contributors:* HangingCurve, StuartCheshire, RxS, Benlisquare, Bgwhite, RadioFan, Hydrargyrum, BorgQueen, SmackBot, Ph7five, Frap, Dl2000, Lenoxus, BeenAroundAWhile, CompRhetoric, Cydebot, Joe Schmedley, RJaguar3, Wikievil666, John Nevard, Eik Corell, Addbot, Fluffernutter, Freikorp, AnomieBOT, Xqbot, FrescoBot, Smile4ever, Eric 324, RedBot, Lotje, RjwilmsiBot, ZéroBot, Medeis, Wingman417, Champion, HandsomeFella, Kenny Strawn, ClueBot NG, Zashitnik, Island Monkey, JasonMashak, The Anonymouse, Zergeist and Anonymous: 19

- **Mac Protector** *Source:* https://en.wikipedia.org/wiki/Mac_Defender?oldid=697222709 *Contributors:* HangingCurve, StuartCheshire, RxS, Benlisquare, Bgwhite, RadioFan, Hydrargyrum, BorgQueen, SmackBot, Ph7five, Frap, Dl2000, Lenoxus, BeenAroundAWhile, CompRhetoric, Cydebot, Joe Schmedley, RJaguar3, Wikievil666, John Nevard, Eik Corell, Addbot, Fluffernutter, Freikorp, AnomieBOT, Xqbot, FrescoBot, Smile4ever, Eric 324, RedBot, Lotje, RjwilmsiBot, ZéroBot, Medeis, Wingman417, Champion, HandsomeFella, Kenny Strawn, ClueBot NG, Zashitnik, Island Monkey, JasonMashak, The Anonymouse, Zergeist and Anonymous: 19

- **Mac Security** *Source:* https://en.wikipedia.org/wiki/Mac_Defender?oldid=697222709 *Contributors:* HangingCurve, StuartCheshire, RxS, Benlisquare, Bgwhite, RadioFan, Hydrargyrum, BorgQueen, SmackBot, Ph7five, Frap, Dl2000, Lenoxus, BeenAroundAWhile, CompRhetoric, Cydebot, Joe Schmedley, RJaguar3, Wikievil666, John Nevard, Eik Corell, Addbot, Fluffernutter, Freikorp, AnomieBOT, Xqbot, FrescoBot, Smile4ever, Eric 324, RedBot, Lotje, RjwilmsiBot, ZéroBot, Medeis, Wingman417, Champion, HandsomeFella, Kenny Strawn, ClueBot NG, Zashitnik, Island Monkey, JasonMashak, The Anonymouse, Zergeist and Anonymous: 19

- **Mac Shield** *Source:* https://en.wikipedia.org/wiki/Mac_Defender?oldid=697222709 *Contributors:* HangingCurve, StuartCheshire, RxS, Benlisquare, Bgwhite, RadioFan, Hydrargyrum, BorgQueen, SmackBot, Ph7five, Frap, Dl2000, Lenoxus, BeenAroundAWhile, CompRhetoric, Cydebot, Joe Schmedley, RJaguar3, Wikievil666, John Nevard, Eik Corell, Addbot, Fluffernutter, Freikorp, AnomieBOT, Xqbot, FrescoBot, Smile4ever, Eric 324, RedBot, Lotje, RjwilmsiBot, ZéroBot, Medeis, Wingman417, Champion, HandsomeFella, Kenny Strawn, ClueBot NG, Zashitnik, Island Monkey, JasonMashak, The Anonymouse, Zergeist and Anonymous: 19

- **MS Antivirus (malware)** *Source:* https://en.wikipedia.org/wiki/MS_Antivirus_(malware)?oldid=696390076 *Contributors:* Damian Yerrick, Edward, Wiwaxia, Xanzzibar, RoyBoy, Arthena, Mattfast1, Drat, Mikeo, Mindmatrix, Tabletop, Graham87, Rjwilmsi, Nneonneo, Aussie Evil, Pip2andahalf, Rgherbert, NawlinWiki, Lockesdonkey, Nentuaby, SmackBot, Michaelcox, Seduisant, OmnipotentEntity, Robofish, JHunterJ, HelloAnnyong, WilliamJE, Jack4740, Eastlaw, FleetCommand, Unionhawk, Seven of Nine, AL16, Neuroelectronic, Dawnseeker2000, SpongeSebastian, Pierre Monteux, Magioladitis, CommonsDelinker, Pharaoh of the Wizards, Supuhstar, Rubricat, Atama, Qu3a, Colintso, Andokool12, CMBJ, Raiden X, Sephiroth storm, Vanished user j3roijqwkskjf5kr, Windowsvistafan, Oxymoron83, Arnos78, Nattelsker, ClueBot, The Thing That Should Not Be, Stepshep, Canis Lupus, Socrates2008, SoxBot, DanielPharos, SF007, Ayjazz, Mikon8er, Pioneer42, Addbot, Speer320, Freakmighty, Medessec, Yongjianrong, MagnusA.Bot, Fluffernutter, Download, Missingno255, Keithieopia, Matt.T, AnomieBOT, Max Cheung, Jim1138, Apollo, Awesomeness, EmpD++, Bihco, Junkcops, Tanarus Asamiya, Ched, A1a33, Mogsworth, Blaster395, Danzon123, Time501, КоЯп, BubbleDude22, Jb577, Tailman8079, AndrewCrogonklol, Thalfon, Marcgal, HamburgerRadio, Vrabu, Seryo93, MrZanzi, Pcuser42, Evosoho, Starbox, DARTH SIDIOUS 2, RjwilmsiBot, EmausBot, Xb0x4lyf3, Techguy197, ZéroBot, Pastore Italy, ClueBot NG, CarrieMJJ, Meltdown627, Mythpage88, Muselovering, Riley Huntley, Security Shield, ChangeEverthing, SirkusSystems, Sourov0000, MasterONEz, Stranger195, DelugeRPG and Anonymous: 87

- **NightMare (scareware)** *Source:* https://en.wikipedia.org/wiki/NightMare_(scareware)?oldid=660826249 *Contributors:* Bearcat, The RedBurn, RocketMaster, Derek R Bullamore, Boleyn, Dthomsen8, Jarble, Yobot, AnomieBOT, Starbox, January, JonMerel, Bilorv, Mrstickman1997 and Anonymous: 2

- **Registry cleaner** *Source:* https://en.wikipedia.org/wiki/Registry_cleaner?oldid=668947230 *Contributors:* Zundark, The Anome, TonyW, EricBright, Xgenei, Bletch, R. S. Shaw, Philip Cross, Mark.Howison, Bsadowski1, Mattbrundage, Plrk, Emops, Rjwilmsi, Ahunt, Bgwhite, Hairy Dude, Hydrargyrum, Janke, Joel7687, Długosz, Ospalh, FlyingPenguins, NorsemanII, Zzuuzz, Simxp, DearPrudence, SmackBot, Ariedartin, Chris the speller, Bluebot, Canoro, Colonies Chris, John Reaves, Frap, Fraser Chapman, Nakon, Rectorrite, Warren, JohnI, Vanisaac, Artificial Silence, FleetCommand, Zarex, Jac16888, Cydebot, DumbBOT, Oerjan, Ragreevy, Fayenatic london, Mariol, Dogru144, Xmido, Rami R, Animum, Xoid, CliffC, Jesant13, Smithkarl, Juliancolton, Tagus, Pogga, Bonadea, Calwiki, Corvus cornix, Registrymaster, Jimmi Hugh, Jasonzbell, Biscuittin, SMC89, RJaguar3, Cosmo0, Lue my, Konamaiki, Chanchowike, Ranaonline, Socrates2008, Bjm0205, Iohannes Animosus, Maynardsantos, Nikados, Morriske, XLinkBot, Kbdankbot, Addbot, Xp54321, Rdavido, Luckas-bot, Brakadabra, AnomieBOT, ThaddeusB, Jim1138, Piano non troppo, Wyayantong, S0aasdf2sf, ArroLu, Alan1000, Catpowerzzz, Lobbslobb, Jglass7268, ATDC Raigeki, Diblidabliduu, Juhko, MrJerry01, Jackfitzgerald, PeterKacz, RjwilmsiBot, Flagins, Sarajensen, ROI ROMAN, Fdr2001, K kisses, Rlithgow, ClueBot NG, Jack Greenmaven, Piyush1992, Helpful Pixie Bot, BG19bot, Toccata quarta, Bgibbs2, Ilovefiledeer, Bardbom, Screwdryver, SimonBirch1973 and Anonymous: 149

- **Rogue security software** *Source:* https://en.wikipedia.org/wiki/Rogue_security_software?oldid=699309888 *Contributors:* Fubar Obfusco, Julesd, WhisperToMe, Mazin07, Senthil, Nurg, Jfire, Vsmith, Bender235, Cwolfsheep, Charonn0, Espoo, Anthony Appleyard, Ron Ritzman, Woohookitty, RHaworth, MyFavoriteMartin, JIP, Rjwilmsi, Koavf, Quietust, Bubba73, Kri, Aussie Evil, NawlinWiki, FlyingPenguins, Real decimic, Nailbiter, Kevin, SmackBot, Jasy jatere, SmackEater, Ohnoitsjamie, RocketMaster, Chris the speller, Improbcat, Trimzulu, JonHarder, Azumanga1, Nakon, Dreadstar, Kukini, Fanx, Cableguytk, Green Giant, JHunterJ, Peyre, TheFarix, Blakegripling ph, RekishiEJ, Cryptic C62, FatalError, Fredvries, CmdrObot, Ivan Pozdeev, Jackzhp, Iuio, Greystork, Davidnason, Sadaphal, DevinCook, Poowis, Jesse Viviano, Seven of Nine, Gogo Dodo, Ameliorate!, Satori Son, Malleus Fatuorum, Nonagonal Spider, Dalahäst, Pogogunner, Obiwankenobi, AjaaniSherisu, Barek, Mark Grant, Geniac, Rhodilee, VoABot II, WikiMax, Michael Goodyear, Schumi555, Inclusivedisjunction, Gwern, CliffC, Falazure, R'n'B, CommonsDelinker, .1337., Pharaoh of the Wizards, Skier Dude, AppleMacReporter, Chaosraiden, TanookiMario257, Talon Kelson, Bonadea, VolkovBot, N3cr0m4nc3r, Philip Trueman, Jart351, Kok3388, Haseo9999, Synthebot, LittleBenW, AlleborgoBot, PedroDaGr8, Raiden X, Malcolmxl5, IHateMalware, Sephiroth storm, Flyer22 Reborn, EwanMclean2005, Es101, Phykyloman~enwiki, Jessejaksin, ClueBot, Chuckbronson45, LizardJr8, Chiazwhiz, Regardless143, Excirial, Socrates2008, Anon lynx, NuclearWarfare, Purplewowies, Autoplayer, Htfiddler, DanielPharos, Callinus, SF007, DumZiBoT, Mikon8er, Ginnrelay, Sigrulfr, Wikiuser100, Jennysue, Texasrexbobcat, Addbot, Xp54321, Trapped34, Flo 1, Smithereen, GastonRabbit, Yobot, Tohd8BohaithuGh1, Marvel Freak, Jponiato, KieranC15, SilverEye-Pro, Killiondude, Obersachsebot, CPU01, Jeffrey Mall, Junkcops, 🔲🔲🔲, A1a33, S0aasdf2sf, КоЯп, BubbleDude22, AndrewCrogonklol, Pre-Cautioned Watcher, Beaconblack, Uvula!, Fastguy397, WPANI, Stars1408, ObbySnadles, HamburgerRadio, Citation bot 1, MaxwellHerme, ASCMSEM1, Jacobdead, Σ, Starbox, MichaelRivers, Deadrat, Lotje, CenSorShot, Kanzler31, Born2bgratis, Spyware exspert, Sky17565292, Ebe123, Progprog, Techguy197, Kunal0315, Napeyga, Champion, Dlowe2224, Ego White Tray, DClason93, Kldukes, Rich Smith, Skylar130, Helpful Pixie Bot, Kinaro, IlSignoreDeiPC, Terryforsdyke, Meatsgains, JC.Torpey, HybridBiology, Farqad, Tangaling, Zeeyanwiki, Codename Lisa, Webclient101, Kephir, Soda drinker, Sourov0000, MasterONEz, Marufsau, PersistedUser, Revantteotia, Logonemeri, Keni and Anonymous: 262

- **Scareware** *Source:* https://en.wikipedia.org/wiki/Scareware?oldid=700730683 *Contributors:* Edward, Andres, Nurg, Xanzzibar, Ebear422, Grm wnr, Andrewferrier, Evice, CanisRufus, Kappa, TheParanoidOne, Jivlain, Kgrr, Mandarax, NeonMerlin, Robert A West, Nentuaby, SmackBot, C.Fred, Robocoder, Breno, Goodnightmush, Sabertooth, Uruiamme, Prolog, Barek, TheOtherSiguy, AlmostReadytoFly, Michael Goodyear, Maurice Carbonaro, DoubleZeta, SovereignGFC, VolkovBot, Fences and windows, TXiKiBoT, Darkrevenger, Jamelan, The Seventh Taylor, Thisismyrofl, LittleBenW, Logan, Moonriddengirl, Alexbot, Socrates2008, Callinus, Mikon8er, Nathan Johnson, ErkinBatu, MystBot, Addbot, Zellfaze, Sillyfolkboy, GastonRabbit, Megaman en m, Luckas-bot, Yobot, UltraMagnus, Metalhead94, Xqbot, Vanished user oweironvoweiuo0239u49regt8j3849hjtowiefj234, 🔲🔲🔲, Cantons-de-l'Est, Tabledhote, FrescoBot, LucienBOT, Haein45, HamburgerRadio, Anonymous07921, Winterst, Starbox, Train2104, Deadrat, Jonkerz, Lotje, Teenboi001, Chris Rocen, WikitanvirBot, Angrytoast, Illogicalpie, Pooh110andco, ZéroBot, Fæ, The Nut, Wabbott9, Staszek Lem, Taistelu-Jaska, DASHBotAV, Roambassador, ClueBot NG, Vibhijain, Northamerica1000, Mccallister8, Flexo013, Security Shield, Farqad, Codename Lisa, Mogism, Sourov0000, 069952497a, Mannir muhammad and Anonymous: 70

- **Spylocked** *Source:* https://en.wikipedia.org/wiki/Spylocked?oldid=644202569 *Contributors:* David.Monniaux, Sus scrofa, Dialectric, FlyingPenguins, Otto ter Haar, SmackBot, Improbcat, Christopher denman, John, Nonagonal Spider, Dancanm, Luna Santin, Ccbanker, Milo03, Fist of Glory, PeterHuber, Kok3388, Cantbuymelove, Mike1d, WJerome, Matthewedwards, John421, Erik Seaberg, Es101, MadmanBot, Brusov, Mp101, CaptainIron555, Socrates2008, 1ForTheMoney, MasterOfTheXP, AnomieBOT, HamburgerRadio, AK456, Oiyarbepsy and Anonymous: 74

- **SpySheriff** *Source:* https://en.wikipedia.org/wiki/SpySheriff?oldid=701166924 *Contributors:* Fubar Obfusco, Edward, WhisperToMe, Bovlb, AliveFreeHappy, Rich Farmbrough, Pearle, Stuartyeates, Marasmusine, Nneonneo, Fish and karate, FlaBot, Aussie Evil, Madkayaker, Kiyosuki, Bachrach44, Aaron Brenneman, Tony1, BazookaJoe, Noclip, SmackBot, ProveIt, SmackEater, Frap, PanicAttack, Red Alien, Peyre, Iridescent, Jestix, Fredvries, KyraVixen, MC10, Mattiator, Sabertooth, Geekosaurus, Marek69, Screen317, Jj137, Spencer, Dreaded Walrus, MER-C, Mullibok, MasterA113, Geniac, Repku, Magioladitis, Bongwarrior, Blanko4, CliffC, Jesant13, AppleMacReporter, AA, KylieTastic, Philip Trueman, WANGXD, Thisismyrofl, WJerome, Rimmington01, Ben4021, Thirteen squared, Phykyloman~enwiki, OwnageDAN, Kanonkas, ImageRemovalBot, Sfan00 IMG, ClueBot, Mr. pesci, MalwareSmarts, VandalRemover, Jesmie1122, Chiazwhiz, Socrates2008, Bozi7, DanielPharos, The Baroness of Morden, PCHS-NJROTC, Mikon8er, Demonspike357, ErkinBatu, MystBot, Addbot, Vatrena ptica, AtheWeatherman, Jasper Deng, Krano, חובבשירה, Yobot, MasterRangi, TwinkleUser, AnomieBOT, Materialscientist, ArthurBot, Junkcops, Vanished user oweironvoweiuo0239u49regt8j3849hjtowiefj234, Pre-Cautioned Watcher, Alexlev55, HamburgerRadio, Vrabu, ISEETRUTH, S-J-S-F-M-W, Heymid, TuneyLoon, Krejcjus393, Taistelu-Jaska, ChuispastonBot, ClueBot NG, BG19bot, IlSignoreDeiPC, Testor Ploa, Crushingkiller, Thepurpledog, RudolfRed, TooSimilar111, Security Shield, Cyberbot II, Theacrosoftn, Dogbig90, Sourov0000, Epicgenius, TheMillionRabbit, BryanWeather, Linuxrox, Babestress, ElectronicKing888, CoolGamer23, ApparatumLover, Yololololoawesome, JJMC89, Tmtabari, DelugeRPG, Ahmedyehia200, Majneeds2chill, Offical Levo Films, Evancahill, Ae9000ae and Anonymous: 133

- **SpywareQuake** *Source:* https://en.wikipedia.org/wiki/SpywareQuake?oldid=666305332 *Contributors:* AxelBoldt, Rpyle731, Dialectric, SmackEater, Xyzzyplugh, Loreanus, Socrates2008, Ronhjones, Yobot, AnomieBOT, Vrabu, HellcatV and Anonymous: 4

- **SpywareStrike** *Source:* https://en.wikipedia.org/wiki/SpySheriff?oldid=701166924 *Contributors:* Fubar Obfusco, Edward, WhisperToMe, Bovlb, AliveFreeHappy, Rich Farmbrough, Pearle, Stuartyeates, Marasmusine, Nneonneo, Fish and karate, FlaBot, Aussie Evil, Madkayaker,

Kiyosuki, Bachrach44, Aaron Brenneman, Tony1, BazookaJoe, Noclip, SmackBot, ProveIt, SmackEater, Frap, PanicAttack, Red Alien, Peyre, Iridescent, Jestix, Fredvries, KyraVixen, MC10, Mattiator, Sabertooth, Geekosaurus, Marek69, Screen317, Jj137, Spencer, Dreaded Walrus, MER-C, Mullibok, MasterA113, Geniac, Repku, Magioladitis, Bongwarrior, Blanko4, CliffC, Jesant13, AppleMacReporter, AA, KylieTastic, Philip Trueman, WANGXD, Thisismyrofl, WJerome, Rimmington01, Ben4021, Thirteen squared, Phykyloman~enwiki, OwnageDAN, Kanonkas, ImageRemovalBot, Sfan00 IMG, ClueBot, Mr. pesci, MalwareSmarts, VandalRemover, Jesmie1122, Chiazwhiz, Socrates2008, Bozi7, DanielPharos, The Baroness of Morden, PCHS-NJROTC, Mikon8er, Demonspike357, ErkinBatu, MystBot, Addbot, Vatrena ptica, AtheWeatherman, Jasper Deng, Krano, חובבשירה, Yobot, MasterRangi, TwinkleUser, AnomieBOT, Materialscientist, ArthurBot, Junkcops, Vanished user oweironvoweiuo0239u49regt8j3849hjtowiefj234, Pre-Cautioned Watcher, Alexlev55, HamburgerRadio, Vrabu, ISEETRUTH, S-J-S-F-M-W, Heymid, TuneyLoon, Krejcjus393, Taistelu-Jaska, ChuispastonBot, ClueBot NG, BG19bot, IlSignoreDeiPC, Testor Ploa, Crushingkiller, Thepurpledog, RudolfRed, TooSimilar111, Security Shield, Cyberbot II, Theacrosoftn, Dogbig90, Sourov0000, Epicgenius, TheMillionRabbit, BryanWeather, Linuxrox, Babestress, ElectronicKing888, CoolGamer23, ApparatumLover, Yololololoawesome, JJMC89, Tmtabari, DelugeRPG, Ahmedyehia200, Majneeds2chill, Offical Levo Films, Evancahill, Ae9000ae and Anonymous: 133

- **Tapsnake** *Source:* https://en.wikipedia.org/wiki/Tapsnake?oldid=655219441 *Contributors:* DragonflySixtyseven, Dthomsen8, Ragityman, GoingBatty, Wgolf and Veryproicelandic

- **ThinkPoint** *Source:* https://en.wikipedia.org/wiki/ThinkPoint?oldid=653637098 *Contributors:* Bearcat, Geni, TPIRFanSteve, Shirt58, ImageRemovalBot, Trivialist, Socrates2008, Carriearchdale, Bearsmalaysia, Junkcops, Kubuswoningen, HamburgerRadio, Colinmurff, Pastore Italy, Dangu123, Yehyaelmasry, Tomp5331, HappyLogolover2011, Kinaro and Anonymous: 12

- **Ultimate Defender** *Source:* https://en.wikipedia.org/wiki/Ultimate_Defender?oldid=566073101 *Contributors:* Fubar Obfusco, SmackBot, Ultraexactzz, Wjmummert, ImageRemovalBot, Socrates2008, DanielPharos, BubbleDude22, FrescoBot, Theo10011, Low Gravitas Area, Sourov0000 and Anonymous: 2

- **Ultimate Fixer** *Source:* https://en.wikipedia.org/wiki/Ultimate_Fixer?oldid=670412365 *Contributors:* Pnm, RJFJR, Jkatzen, Dialectric, Ultraexactzz, Alaibot, Dylan anglada, Squids and Chips, Lottiotta, Ratchet12345, Socrates2008, DanielPharos, Fiftyquid, Yobot, AnomieBOT, Cavarrone, HamburgerRadio, Miszatomic and Anonymous: 4

- **UltimateCleaner** *Source:* https://en.wikipedia.org/wiki/UltimateCleaner?oldid=629328464 *Contributors:* SmackBot, Stifle, Widefox, MER-C, Funandtrvl, VolkovBot, Thisismyrofl, John lanuza2003, Socrates2008, DanielPharos, Addbot, Yobot, Mynameinc, HamburgerRadio, DrilBot, A520, NKMagic221 and Anonymous: 7

- **VirusProtectPro** *Source:* https://en.wikipedia.org/wiki/VirusProtectPro?oldid=575319397 *Contributors:* SmackEater, Blakegripling ph, CliffC, Macy, CompyExpert0001, Benderrocks2007, Auntof6, Socrates2008, DanielPharos, Grikipedia, Fivexthethird, LuK3, Yobot, Killiondude, A1a33, DrilBot, Sourov0000 and Anonymous: 9

- **WinFixer** *Source:* https://en.wikipedia.org/wiki/WinFixer?oldid=699648524 *Contributors:* AxelBoldt, Edward, Harry Wood, Peter Damian (original account), Francs2000, Jredmond, Nurg, Monkeyman, Stepp-Wulf, ESkog, Flapdragon, Mr. Billion, Hurricane111, Cwolfsheep, Joylock, Pearle, Ynhockey, Velella, MadiZone, RJFJR, H2g2bob, JarlaxleArtemis, Fred J, Damienm4, Rjwilmsi, Voretus, Nneonneo, Yamamoto Ichiro, RainR, Alphachimp, Consumed Crustacean, ApolloBoy, Exe, Mrschimpf, Mongreilf, UkPaolo, Splintercellguy, Kinneyboy90, Crazytales, Stephenb, Quentin Smith, Akhristov, Dialectric, Vivaldi, FlyingPenguins, Nacimota, Reyk, Petri Krohn, JLaTondre, Wikipeditor, Cromag, Katieh5584, Jeff Silvers, SmackBot, Gary Kirk, Stifle, Sigmund~enwiki, Mdd4696, Brossow, HalfShadow, KingRaptor, Improbcat, Bluebot, Ezriilc, Spectrechris, Can't sleep, clown will eat me, Noir~enwiki, Frap, OrphanBot, OSborn, Jax9999, Teehee123, Fragnal, Pemu, EdGl, Crd721, Homo sapiens, Vildricianus, Kurt000, ONX, Navin Shetty Brahmavar, Fontenot 1031, Stratadrake, Fredil Yupigo, Blakegripling ph, Octane, Fredvries, Wolfdog, DangerousPanda, CmdrObot, GollyG, INVERTED, Sopoforic, Hydraton31, Ogmios01, Ahezhara, Mario scolas, Geekosaurus, UberScienceNerd, Supermario99, Lår-ilt~enwiki, ChristineDelusion, Peter Eisenburger, Invitatious, Elcasiegno, Sir Simon Tolhurst, Deku-Scrub, Danger, StevenT1, Qwerty Binary, Dreaded Walrus, MER-C, BCube, Geniac, Xsystems, Dboyz-x.etown, Ompd, Nyttend, Knoveau, Achard, CliffC, COstop, Manticore, J.delanoy, AstroHurricane001, TheMeno, Raistlin11325, TubeBaum, WikiChip, 4granite, Netseekers, Joshua Issac, STBotD, Remember the dot, Btdurant, Deor, Kyle the bot, Jedravent, Easel3, Q Science, Kok3388, Haseo9999, WJetChao, Iceshark7, Mike1d, Sephiroth storm, Robert - Northern VA, Es101, Soulweaver, Phykyloman~enwiki, Yoshi225, ImageRemovalBot, Doomdragonz, Ebright82, ClueBot, Muhammadsb1, Fyyer, The Thing That Should Not Be, Geobronx, Griffin006, Socrates2008, Eeekster, Sajith90, DanielPharos, Versus22, Jnw222, PCHS-NJROTC, Ginbot86, DumZiBoT, Mikon8er, Cunard, Addbot, Download, Evildeathmath, Iberium, Missingno255, Tohd8BohaithuGh1, Worm That Turned, USAJAP1, Junkcops, WPANI, Oldlaptop321, A little insignificant, HamburgerRadio, Jonesey95, Nick Rizza, Evosoho, NortyNort, JV Smithy, EmausBot, John of Reading, Beta M, Joines.M, Splibubay, WiiRocks566, ClueBot NG, BattyBot, Cyberbot II, Hmainsbot1, Sourov0000, MustardBlast and Anonymous: 227

25.9.2 Images

- **File:Ambox_important.svg** *Source:* https://upload.wikimedia.org/wikipedia/commons/b/b4/Ambox_important.svg *License:* Public domain *Contributors:* Own work, based off of Image:Ambox scales.svg *Original artist:* Dsmurat (talk · contribs)

- **File:Crystal_Clear_device_cdrom_unmount.png** *Source:* https://upload.wikimedia.org/wikipedia/commons/1/10/Crystal_Clear_device_cdrom_unmount.png *License:* LGPL *Contributors:* All Crystal Clear icons were posted by the author as LGPL on kde-look; *Original artist:* Everaldo Coelho and YellowIcon;

- **File:Edit-clear.svg** *Source:* https://upload.wikimedia.org/wikipedia/en/f/f2/Edit-clear.svg *License:* Public domain *Contributors:* The *Tango!* Desktop Project. *Original artist:*
  The people from the Tango! project. And according to the meta-data in the file, specifically: "Andreas Nilsson, and Jakub Steiner (although minimally)."

- **File:Internet_map_1024.jpg** *Source:* https://upload.wikimedia.org/wikipedia/commons/d/d2/Internet_map_1024.jpg *License:* CC BY 2.5 *Contributors:* Originally from the English Wikipedia; description page is/was here. *Original artist:* The Opte Project

- **File:M_box.svg** *Source:* https://upload.wikimedia.org/wikipedia/commons/9/94/M_box.svg *License:* Public domain *Contributors:* Own work based on: File:Microsoft.svg *Original artist:* Ariesk47 (<a href='//commons.wikimedia.org/wiki/User_talk:Ariesk47' title='User talk:Ariesk47'>talk</a>)

- **File:Malware_logo.svg** *Source:* https://upload.wikimedia.org/wikipedia/commons/f/ff/Malware_logo.svg *License:* LGPL *Contributors:* Skull and crossbones.svg (valid SVG)

  Original artist: Skull and crossbones.svg: Silsor

- **File:Merge-arrow.svg** *Source:* https://upload.wikimedia.org/wikipedia/commons/a/aa/Merge-arrow.svg *License:* Public domain *Contributors:* ? *Original artist:* ?

- **File:Mergefrom.svg** *Source:* https://upload.wikimedia.org/wikipedia/commons/0/0f/Mergefrom.svg *License:* Public domain *Contributors:* ? *Original artist:* ?

- **File:Monitor_padlock.svg** *Source:* https://upload.wikimedia.org/wikipedia/commons/7/73/Monitor_padlock.svg *License:* CC BY-SA 3.0 *Contributors:* Transferred from en.wikipedia; transferred to Commons by User:Logan using CommonsHelper. *Original artist:* Lunarbunny (talk). Original uploader was Lunarbunny at en.wikipedia

- **File:NightMare_Amiga_scareware.png** *Source:* https://upload.wikimedia.org/wikipedia/commons/8/8b/NightMare_Amiga_scareware.png *License:* CC BY-SA 3.0 *Contributors:* Own work *Original artist:* The RedBurn

- **File:Question_book-new.svg** *Source:* https://upload.wikimedia.org/wikipedia/en/9/99/Question_book-new.svg *License:* Cc-by-sa-3.0 *Contributors:*

  Created from scratch in Adobe Illustrator. Based on Image:Question book.png created by User:Equazcion *Original artist:* Tkgd2007

- **File:SSSS_-_SpySheriffScreenShot.jpg** *Source:* https://upload.wikimedia.org/wikipedia/en/a/a5/SSSS_-_SpySheriffScreenShot.jpg *License:* Fair use *Contributors:*

  http://www.bleepingcomputer.com/forums/topic22402.html *Original artist:* ?

- **File:SpySheriffPopUp.png** *Source:* https://upload.wikimedia.org/wikipedia/en/b/bd/SpySheriffPopUp.png *License:* ? *Contributors:* http://vil.nai.com/vil/content/v_135033.htm *Original artist:* ?

- **File:Spysheriff1.png** *Source:* https://upload.wikimedia.org/wikipedia/en/4/43/Spysheriff1.png *License:* Fair use *Contributors:* The user who created the jpeg version of the image: SpySheriff1.jpg. The file is non-existent anymore. *Original artist:* ?

- **File:SpywareProtect09block.PNG** *Source:* https://upload.wikimedia.org/wikipedia/en/4/46/SpywareProtect09block.PNG *License:* Fair use *Contributors:* Screenshot captured on machine infected by MS Antivirus (malware) *Original artist:* ?

- **File:Text_document_with_red_question_mark.svg** *Source:* https://upload.wikimedia.org/wikipedia/commons/a/a4/Text_document_with_red_question_mark.svg *License:* Public domain *Contributors:* Created by bdesham with Inkscape; based upon Text-x-generic.svg from the Tango project. *Original artist:* Benjamin D. Esham (bdesham)

- **File:Wiki_letter_w.svg** *Source:* https://upload.wikimedia.org/wikipedia/en/6/6c/Wiki_letter_w.svg *License:* Cc-by-sa-3.0 *Contributors:* ? *Original artist:* ?

- **File:WinAntiVirus_Pop-Up.png** *Source:* https://upload.wikimedia.org/wikipedia/en/2/22/WinAntiVirus_Pop-Up.png *License:* Fair use *Contributors:* Dialog box created by Opera *Original artist:* ?

- **File:Winfixer-message.png** *Source:* https://upload.wikimedia.org/wikipedia/en/5/56/Winfixer-message.png *License:* ? *Contributors:* ? *Original artist:* ?

- **File:Winfixer.jpg** *Source:* https://upload.wikimedia.org/wikipedia/en/c/c4/Winfixer.jpg *License:* Fair use *Contributors:* http://www.whois.sc/winfixer.com *Original artist:* ?

25.9.3   Content license

www.ingramcontent.com/pod-product-compliance
Lightning Source LLC
Chambersburg PA
CBHW060457060326
40689CB00020B/4564